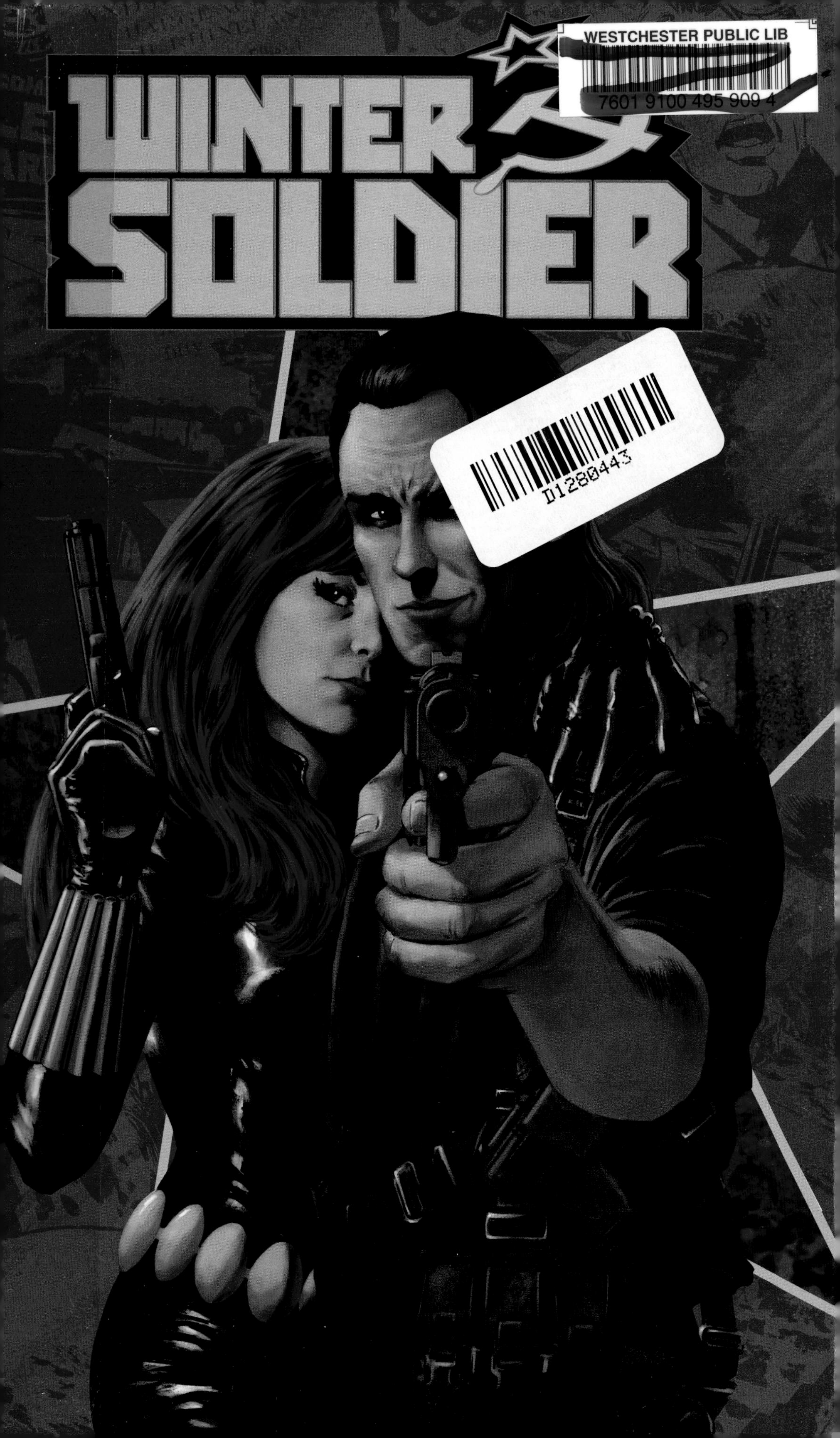
WINTER
SOLDIER

WINTER SOLDIER

BROKEN ARROW

WRITER
ED BRUBAKER

ARTIST
MICHAEL LARK

INKERS
BRIAN THIES WITH STEFANO GAUDIANO

COLOR ARTIST **BETTIE BREITWEISER**
WITH **MITCH BREITWEISER** (#8)

LETTERER **VC'S JOE CARAMAGNA**

COVER ART **STEVE EPTING**

ASSISTANT EDITORS **JOHN DENNING & JAKE THOMAS**

EDITOR **LAUREN SANKOVITCH**

EXECUTIVE EDITOR **TOM BREVOORT**

COLLECTION EDITOR JENNIFER GRÜNWALD
ASSISTANT EDITORS ALEX STARBUCK & NELSON RIBEIRO
EDITOR, SPECIAL PROJECTS MARK D. BEAZLEY
SENIOR EDITOR, SPECIAL PROJECTS JEFF YOUNGQUIST
SENIOR VICE PRESIDENT OF SALES DAVID GABRIEL
SVP OF BRAND PLANNING & COMMUNICATIONS MICHAEL PASCIULLO
BOOK DESIGN JEFF POWELL

EDITOR IN CHIEF AXEL ALONSO
CHIEF CREATIVE OFFICER JOE QUESADA
PUBLISHER DAN BUCKLEY
EXECUTIVE PRODUCER ALAN FINE

WINTER SOLDIER VOL. 2: BROKEN ARROW. Contains material originally published in magazine form as WINTER SOLDIER #6-9. First printing 2012. ISBN# 978-0-7851-4405-2. Published by MARVEL WORLDWIDE, INC., a subsidiary of MARVEL ENTERTAINMENT, LLC. OFFICE OF PUBLICATION: 135 West 50th Street, New York, NY 10020. Copyright © 2012 Marvel Characters, Inc. All rights reserved. $15.99 per copy in the U.S. and $17.99 in Canada (GST #R127032852); Canadian Agreement #40668537. All characters featured in this issue and the distinctive names and likenesses thereof, and all related indicia are trademarks of Marvel Characters, Inc. No similarity between any of the names, characters, persons, and/or institutions in this magazine with those of any living or dead person or institution is intended, and any such similarity which may exist is purely coincidental. **Printed in the U.S.A.** ALAN FINE, EVP - Office of the President, Marvel Worldwide, Inc. and EVP & CMO Marvel Characters B.V.; DAN BUCKLEY, Publisher & President - Print, Animation & Digital Divisions; JOE QUESADA, Chief Creative Officer; TOM BREVOORT, SVP of Publishing; DAVID BOGART, SVP of Operations & Procurement, Publishing; RUWAN JAYATILLEKE, SVP & Associate Publisher, Publishing; C.B. CEBULSKI, SVP of Creator & Content Development; DAVID GABRIEL, SVP of Publishing Sales & Circulation; MICHAEL PASCIULLO, SVP of Brand Planning & Communications; JIM O'KEEFE, VP of Operations & Logistics; DAN CARR, Executive Director of Publishing Technology; SUSAN CRESPI, Editorial Operations Manager; ALEX MORALES, Publishing Operations Manager; STAN LEE, Chairman Emeritus. For information regarding advertising in Marvel Comics or on Marvel.com, please contact Niza Disla, Director of Marvel Partnerships, at ndisla@marvel.com. For Marvel subscription inquiries, please call 800-217-9158. **Manufactured between 10/11/2012 and 11/13/2012 by QUAD/GRAPHICS, DUBUQUE, IA, USA.**

10 9 8 7 6 5 4 3 2 1

CAPTAIN AMERICA'S SIDEKICK JAMES "BUCKY" BARNES DIED IN ACTION
IN THE CLOSING DAYS OF WORLD WAR II , ONLY TO BE RESURRECTED
BY DEPARTMENT X, THE SOVIET UNION'S SECRET SCIENCE DIVISION,
AND BRAINWASHED TO BE THEIR PERFECT COLD WAR ASSASSIN —
THE WINTER SOLDIER! BUT WHEN HIS FORMER PARTNER SAVED HIM
AND RESTORED HIS MEMORIES, HIS TROUBLES TRULY BEGAN...NOW
BELIEVED DEAD BY THE WORLD AT LARGE, AND HAUNTED BY HIS PAST,
BUCKY BARNES FIGHTS FOR REDEMPTION AS THE...

6

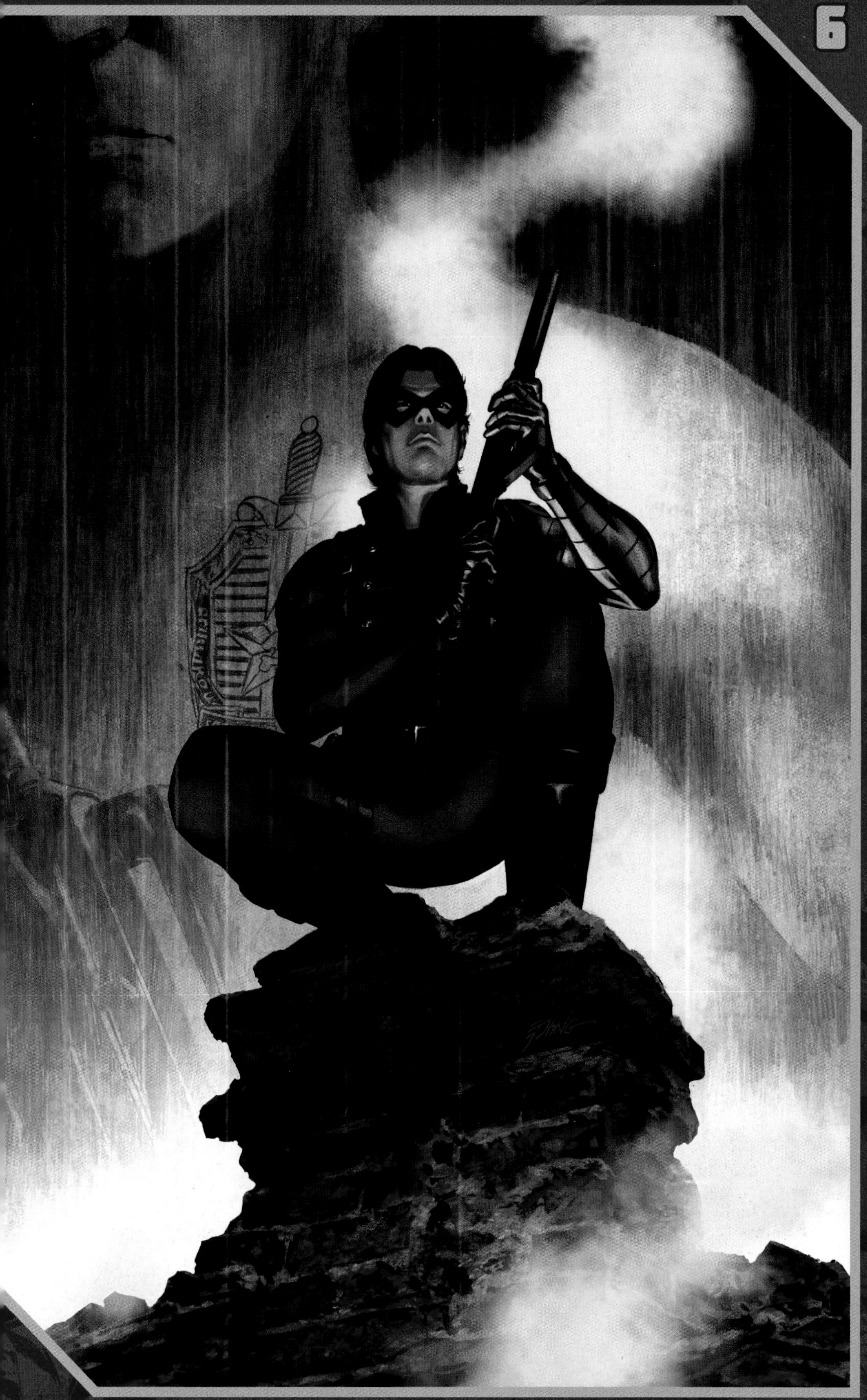

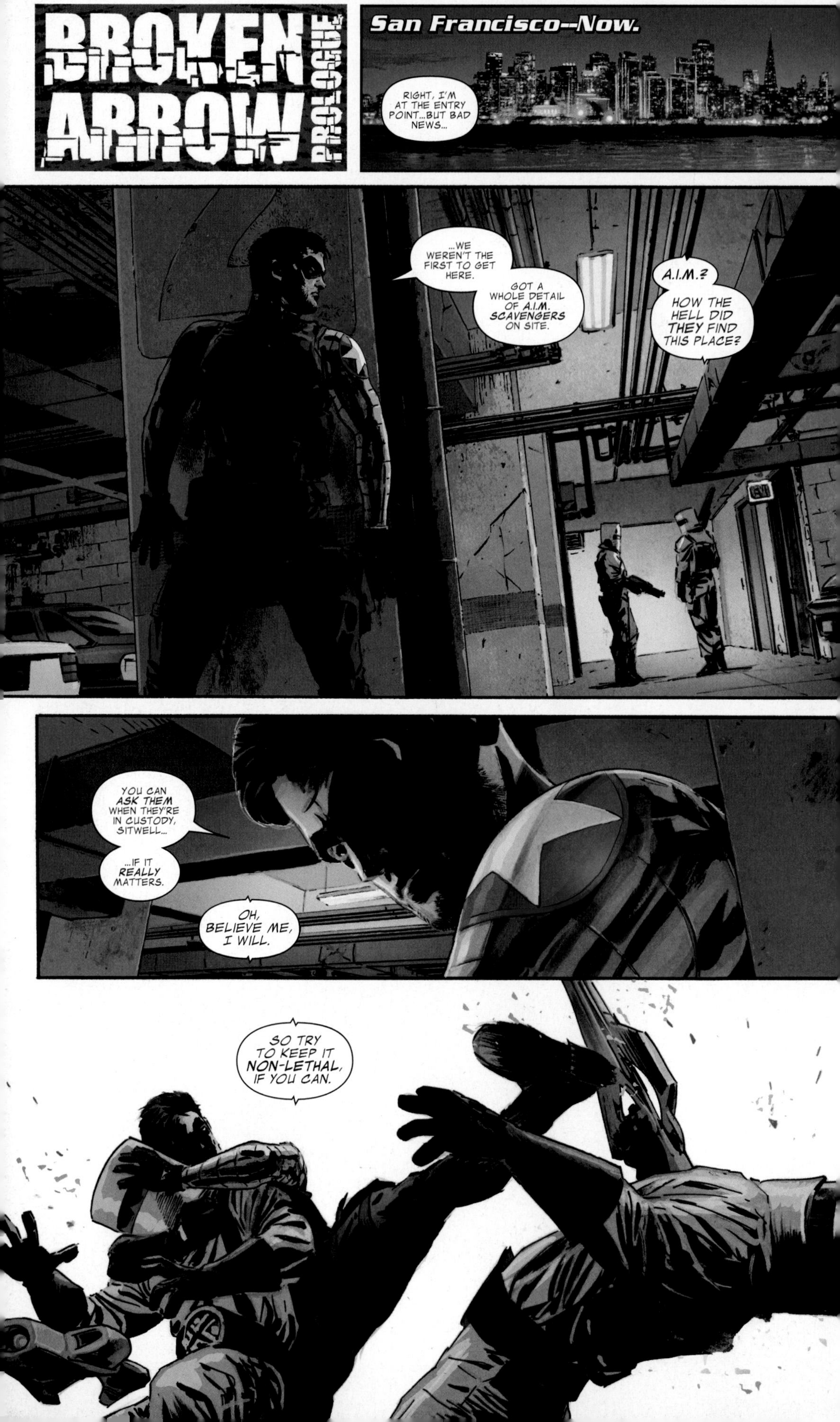
BROKEN ARROW PROLOGUE
San Francisco--Now.
RIGHT, I'M AT THE ENTRY POINT...BUT BAD NEWS...
...WE WEREN'T THE FIRST TO GET HERE.
GOT A WHOLE DETAIL OF A.I.M. SCAVENGERS ON SITE.
A.I.M.?
HOW THE HELL DID THEY FIND THIS PLACE?
YOU CAN ASK THEM WHEN THEY'RE IN CUSTODY, SITWELL...
...IF IT REALLY MATTERS.
OH, BELIEVE ME, I WILL.
SO TRY TO KEEP IT NON-LETHAL, IF YOU CAN.

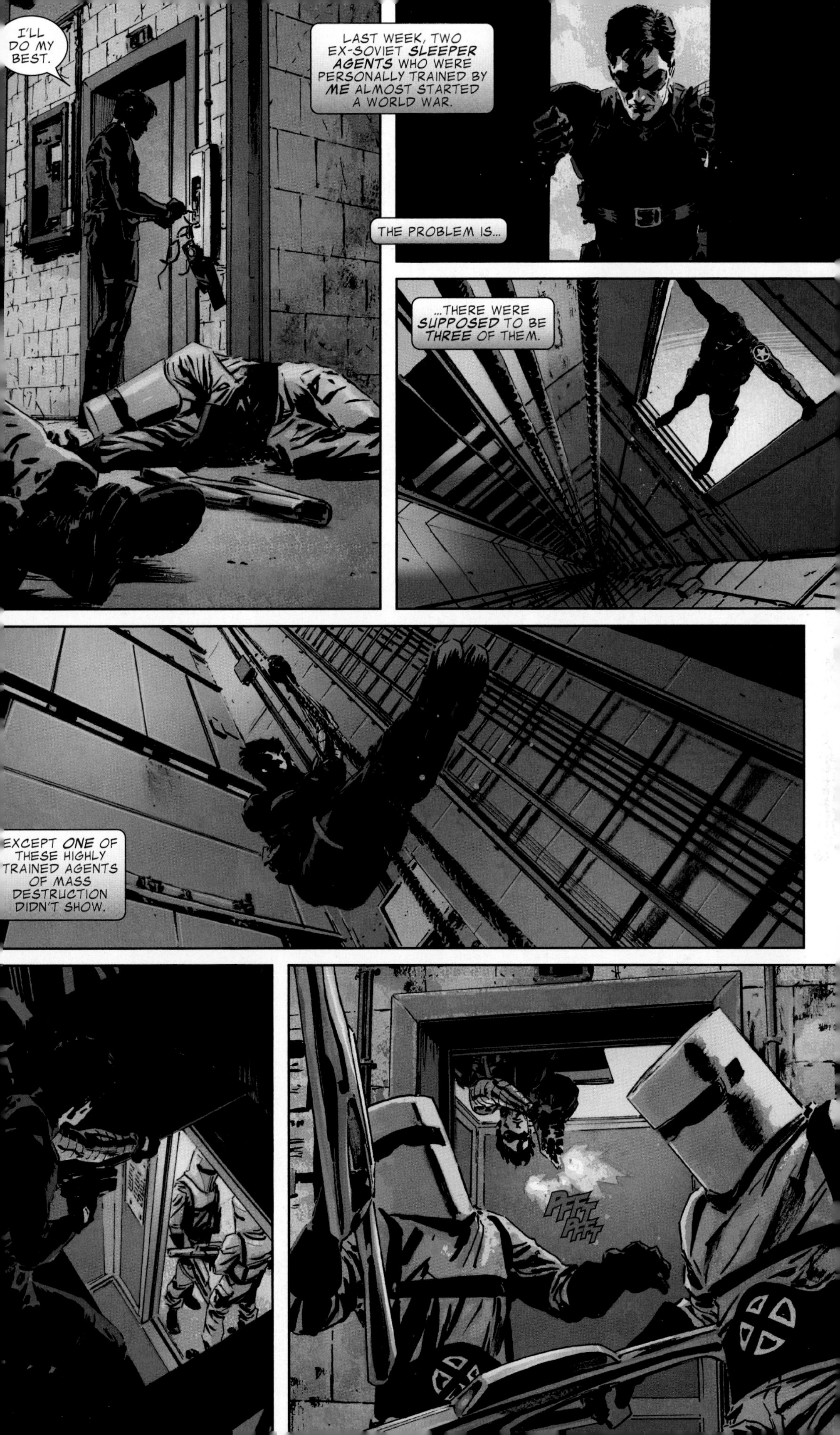
I'LL DO MY BEST.
LAST WEEK, TWO EX-SOVIET SLEEPER AGENTS WHO WERE PERSONALLY TRAINED BY ME ALMOST STARTED A WORLD WAR.
THE PROBLEM IS...
...THERE WERE SUPPOSED TO BE THREE OF THEM.
EXCEPT ONE OF THESE HIGHLY TRAINED AGENTS OF MASS DESTRUCTION DIDN'T SHOW.
PFFT PFFT

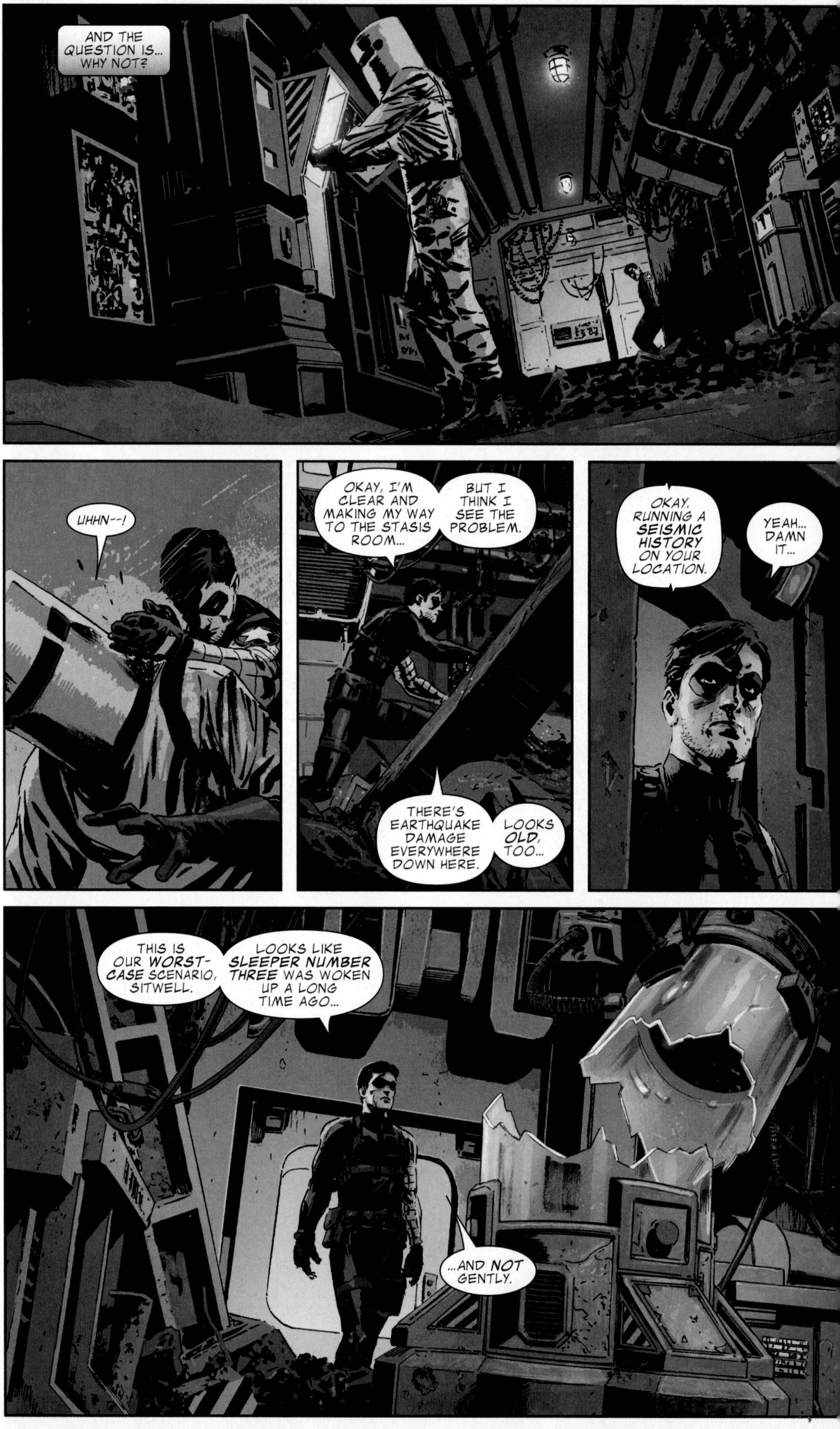
AND THE QUESTION IS... WHY NOT?
UHHN--!
OKAY, I'M CLEAR AND MAKING MY WAY TO THE STASIS ROOM...
BUT I THINK I SEE THE PROBLEM.
THERE'S EARTHQUAKE DAMAGE EVERYWHERE DOWN HERE.
LOOKS OLD, TOO...
OKAY. RUNNING A SEISMIC HISTORY ON YOUR LOCATION.
YEAH... DAMN IT...
THIS IS OUR WORST-CASE SCENARIO, SITWELL.
LOOKS LIKE SLEEPER NUMBER THREE WAS WOKEN UP A LONG TIME AGO...
...AND NOT GENTLY.

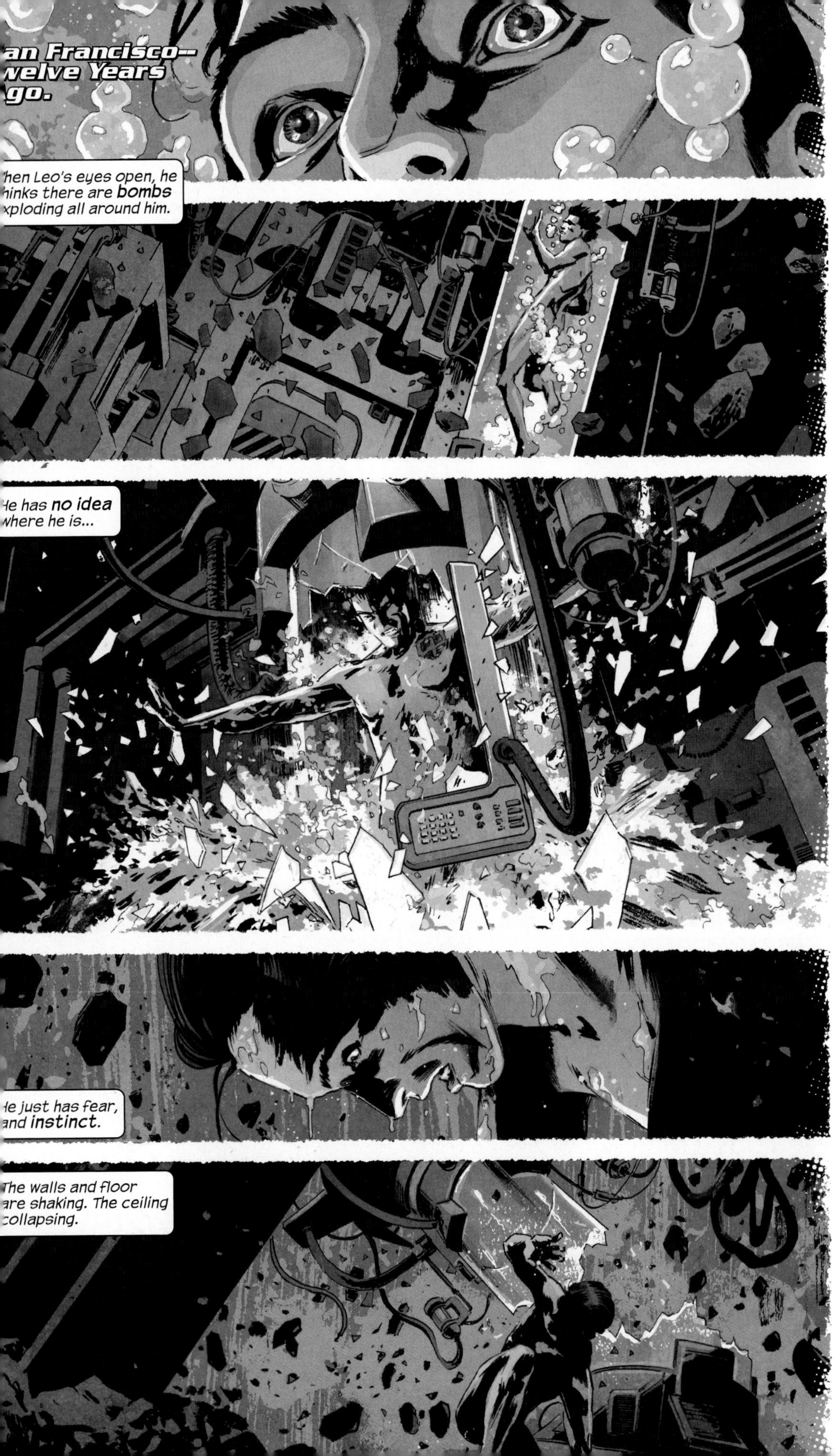
an Francisco--
welve Years
go.
hen Leo's eyes open, he
hinks there are bombs
xploding all around him.
He has no idea
where he is...
He just has fear,
and instinct.
The walls and floor
are shaking. The ceiling
collapsing.

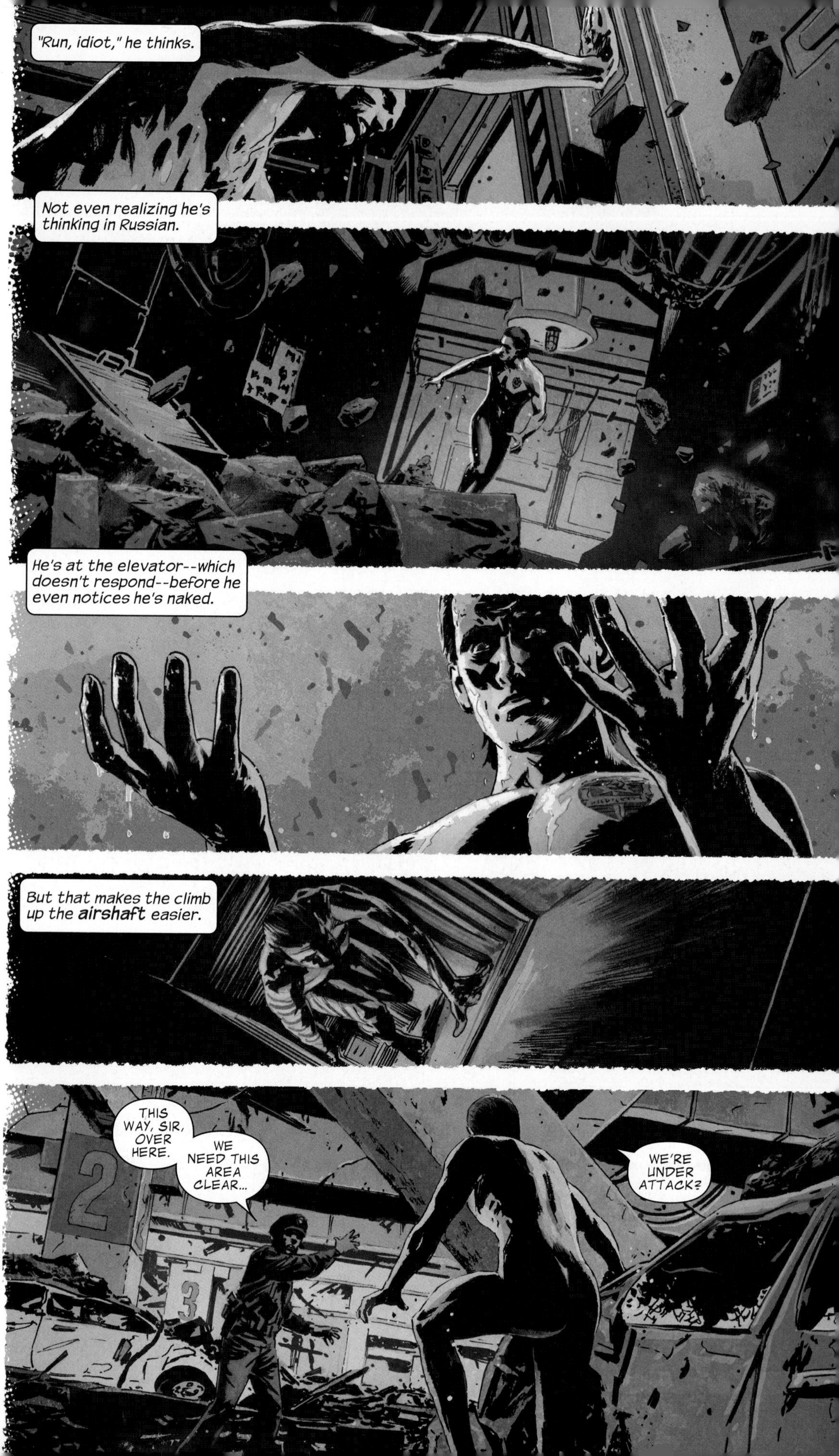
"Run, idiot," he thinks.
Not even realizing he's thinking in Russian.
He's at the elevator--which doesn't respond--before he even notices he's naked.
But that makes the climb up the airshaft easier.
THIS WAY, SIR, OVER HERE.
WE NEED THIS AREA CLEAR...
WE'RE UNDER ATTACK?

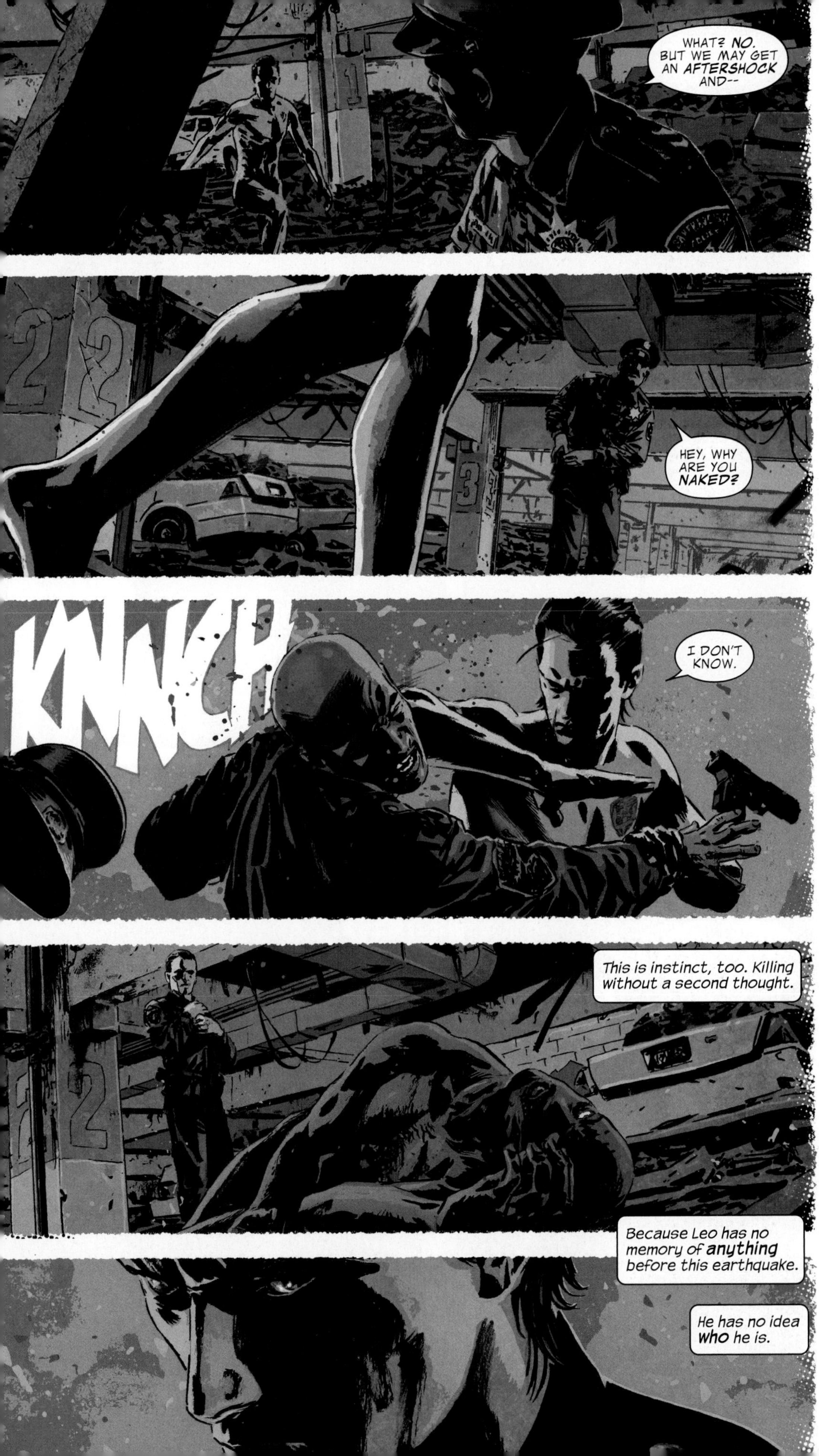
WHAT? NO. BUT WE MAY GET AN AFTERSHOCK AND--
HEY, WHY ARE YOU NAKED?
KNNCH
I DON'T KNOW.
This is instinct, too. Killing without a second thought.
Because Leo has no memory of anything before this earthquake.
He has no idea who he is.

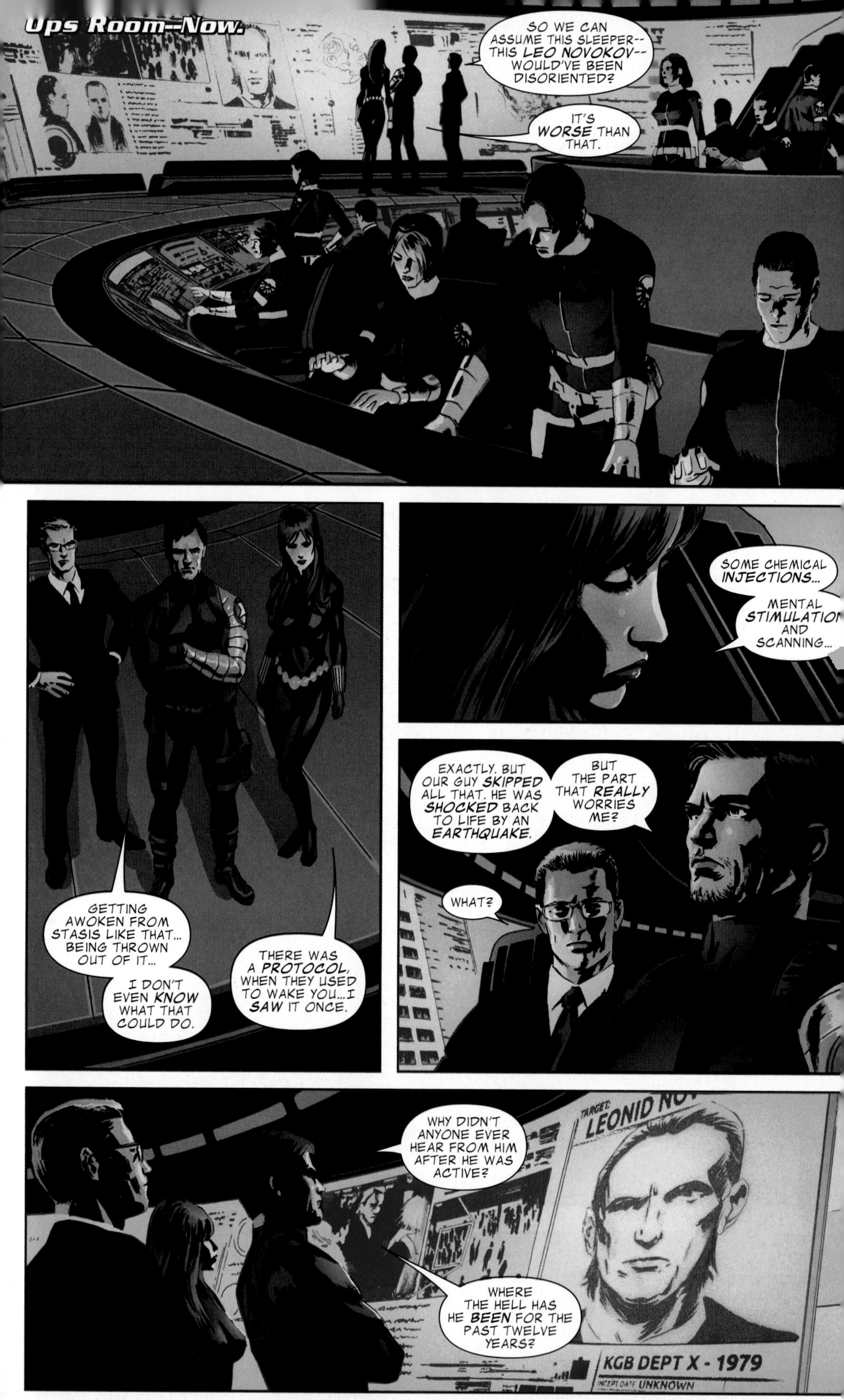

Ops Room--Now.
SO WE CAN ASSUME THIS SLEEPER-- THIS LEO NOVOKOV-- WOULD'VE BEEN DISORIENTED?
IT'S WORSE THAN THAT.
GETTING AWOKEN FROM STASIS LIKE THAT... BEING THROWN OUT OF IT...
I DON'T EVEN KNOW WHAT THAT COULD DO.
THERE WAS A PROTOCOL, WHEN THEY USED TO WAKE YOU...I SAW IT ONCE.
SOME CHEMICAL INJECTIONS...
MENTAL STIMULATION AND SCANNING...
EXACTLY. BUT OUR GUY SKIPPED ALL THAT. HE WAS SHOCKED BACK TO LIFE BY AN EARTHQUAKE.
BUT THE PART THAT REALLY WORRIES ME?
WHAT?
WHY DIDN'T ANYONE EVER HEAR FROM HIM AFTER HE WAS ACTIVE?
TARGET: LEONID NO
WHERE THE HELL HAS HE BEEN FOR THE PAST TWELVE YEARS?
KGB DEPT X - 1979
INCEPT DATE UNKNOWN

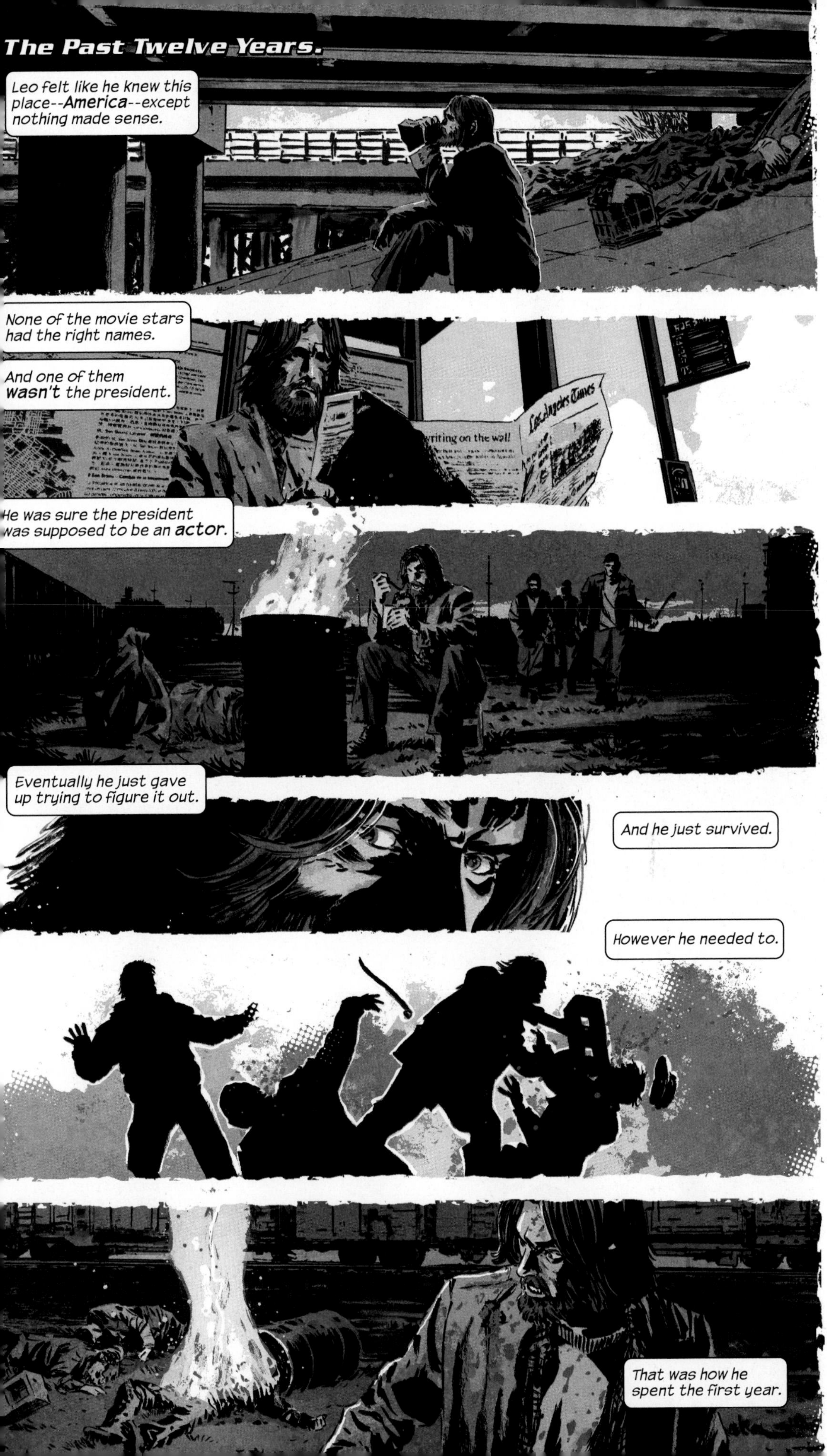
The Past Twelve Years.
Leo felt like he knew this place--America--except nothing made sense.
None of the movie stars had the right names.
And one of them wasn't the president.
writing on the wall!
Los Angeles Times
He was sure the president was supposed to be an actor.
Eventually he just gave up trying to figure it out.
And he just survived.
However he needed to.
That was how he spent the first year.

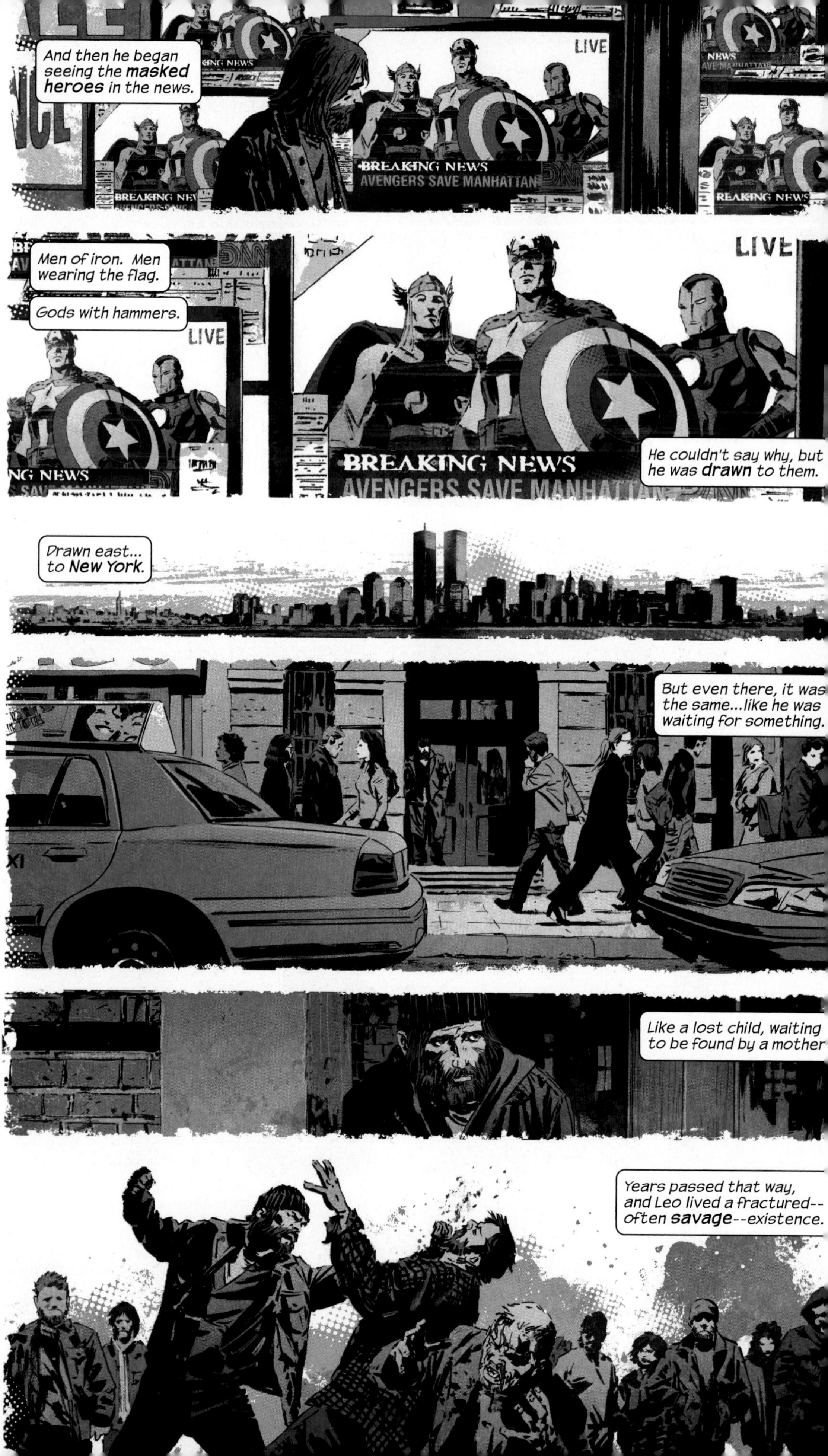
And then he began seeing the **masked heroes** in the news.
LIVE
BREAKING NEWS
AVENGERS SAVE MANHATTAN
Men of iron. Men wearing the flag.
Gods with hammers.
LIVE
LIVE
BREAKING NEWS
AVENGERS SAVE MANHATTAN
He couldn't say why, but he was **drawn** to them.
Drawn east... to **New York**.
But even there, it was the same...like he was waiting for something.
Like a lost child, waiting to be found by a mother
Years passed that way, and Leo lived a fractured--often **savage**--existence.

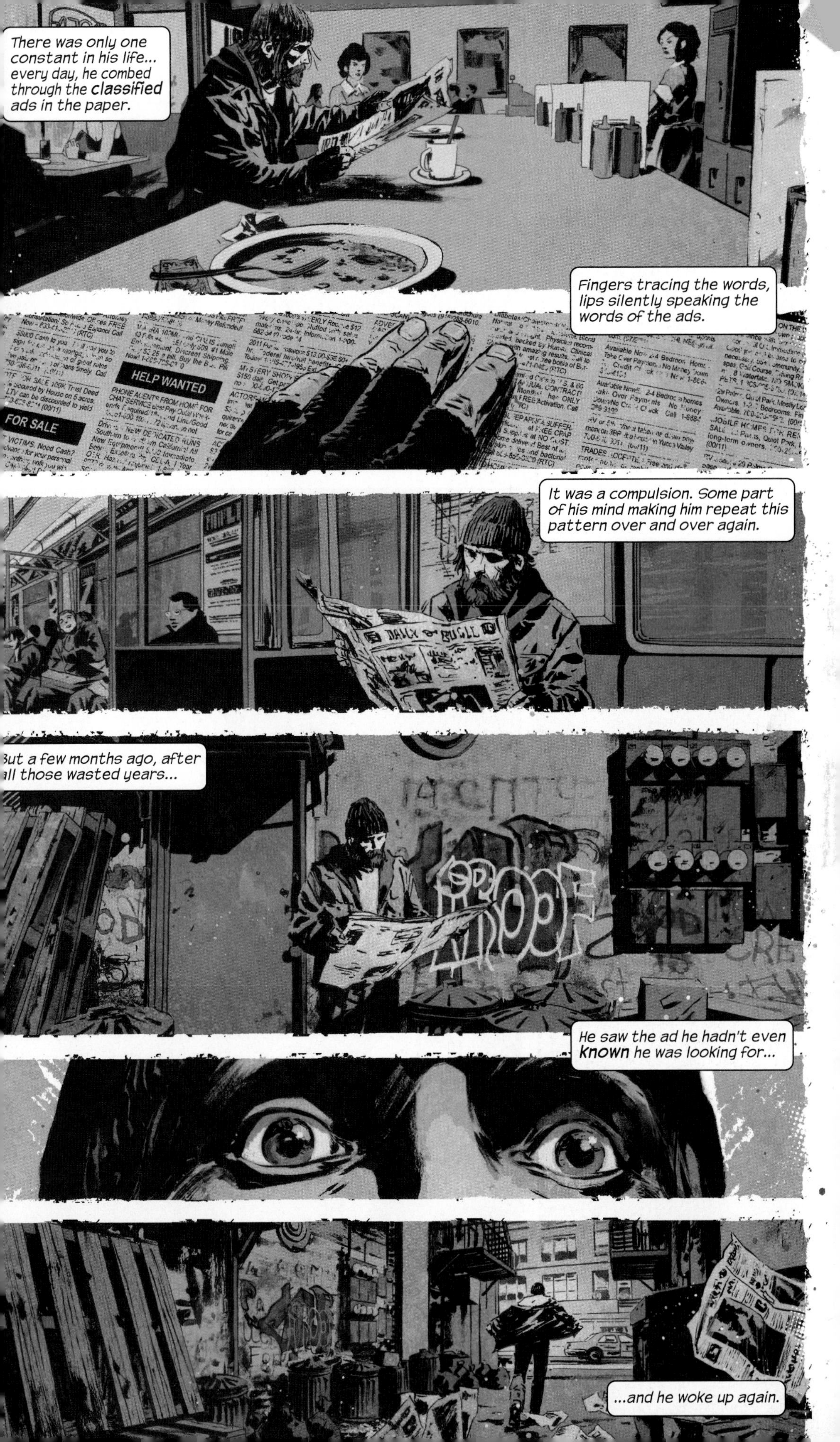
There was only one constant in his life... every day, he combed through the **classified** ads in the paper.
Fingers tracing the words, lips silently speaking the words of the ads.
HELP WANTED
FOR SALE
It was a compulsion. Some part of his mind making him repeat this pattern over and over again.
But a few months ago, after all those wasted years...
He saw the ad he hadn't even **known** he was looking for...
...and he woke up again.

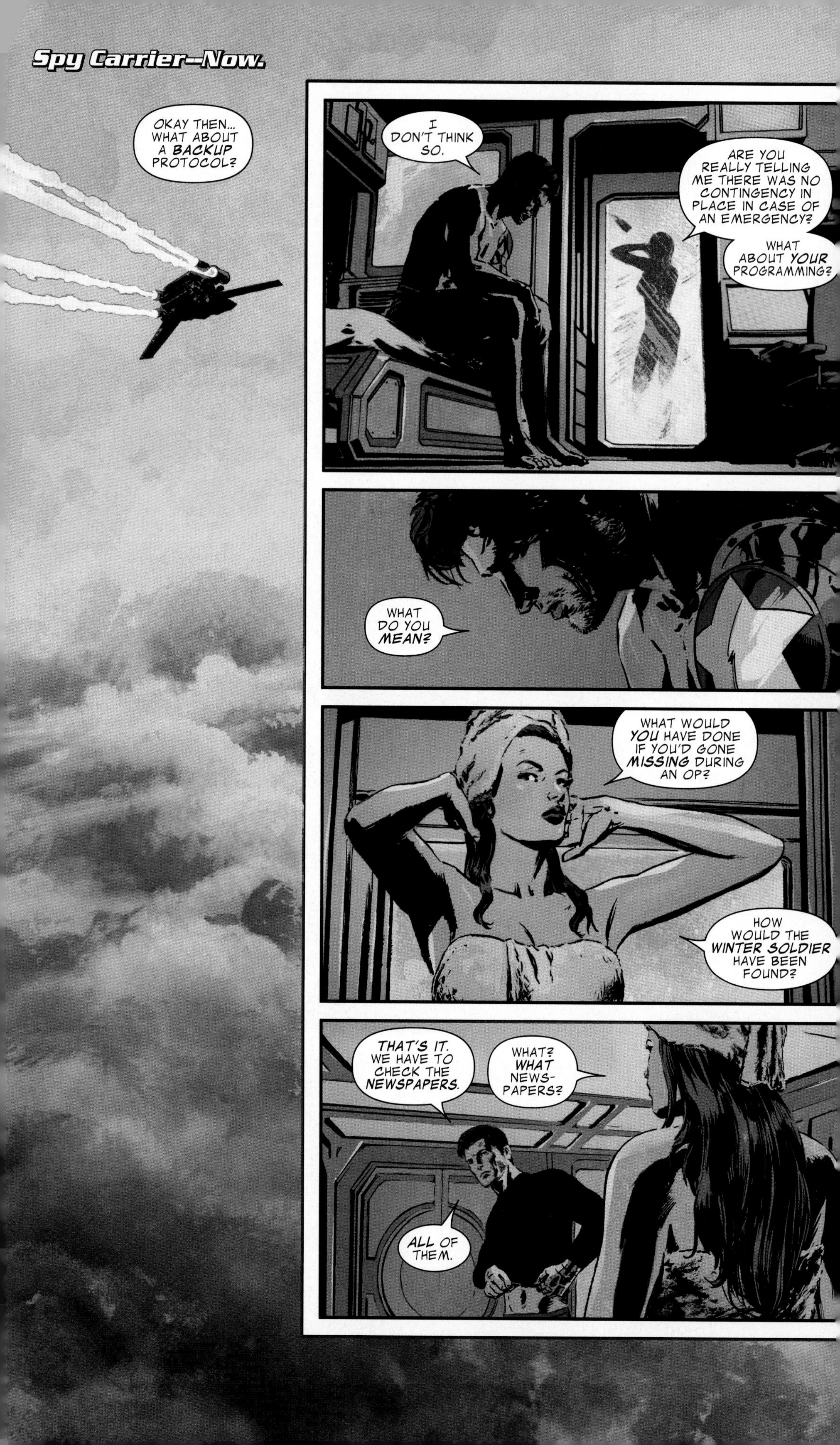
Spy Carrier--Now.
OKAY THEN... WHAT ABOUT A BACKUP PROTOCOL?
I DON'T THINK SO.
ARE YOU REALLY TELLING ME THERE WAS NO CONTINGENCY IN PLACE IN CASE OF AN EMERGENCY?
WHAT ABOUT YOUR PROGRAMMING?
WHAT DO YOU MEAN?
WHAT WOULD YOU HAVE DONE IF YOU'D GONE MISSING DURING AN OP?
HOW WOULD THE WINTER SOLDIER HAVE BEEN FOUND?
THAT'S IT. WE HAVE TO CHECK THE NEWSPAPERS.
WHAT? WHAT NEWS-PAPERS?
ALL OF THEM.

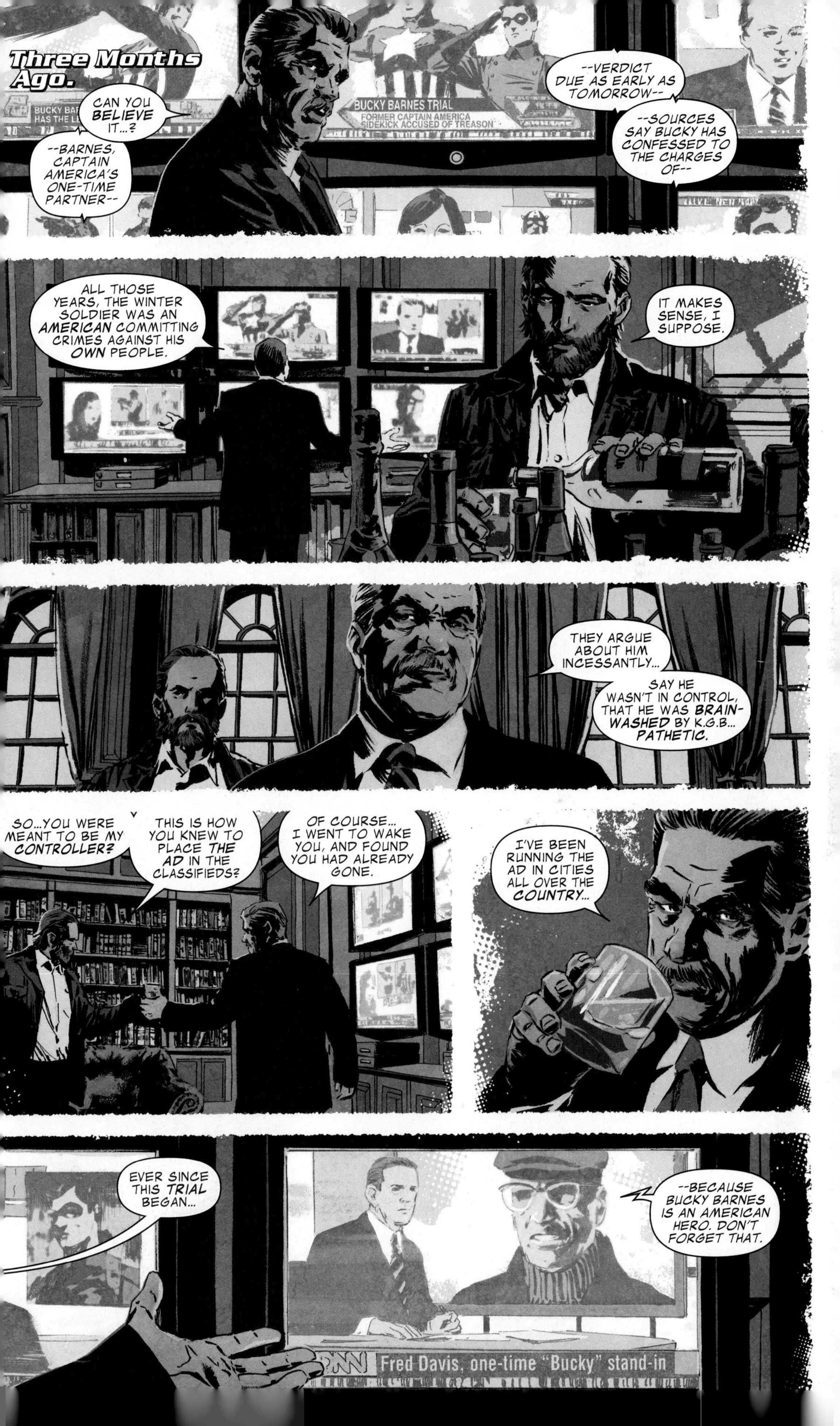

Three Months Ago.
BUCKY BARNES TRIAL
FORMER CAPTAIN AMERICA SIDEKICK ACCUSED OF TREASON
CAN YOU BELIEVE IT...?
--BARNES, CAPTAIN AMERICA'S ONE-TIME PARTNER--
--VERDICT DUE AS EARLY AS TOMORROW--
--SOURCES SAY BUCKY HAS CONFESSED TO THE CHARGES OF--
ALL THOSE YEARS, THE WINTER SOLDIER WAS AN AMERICAN COMMITTING CRIMES AGAINST HIS OWN PEOPLE.
IT MAKES SENSE, I SUPPOSE.
THEY ARGUE ABOUT HIM INCESSANTLY...
SAY HE WASN'T IN CONTROL, THAT HE WAS BRAIN-WASHED BY K.G.B... PATHETIC.
SO...YOU WERE MEANT TO BE MY CONTROLLER?
THIS IS HOW YOU KNEW TO PLACE THE AD IN THE CLASSIFIEDS?
OF COURSE... I WENT TO WAKE YOU, AND FOUND YOU HAD ALREADY GONE.
I'VE BEEN RUNNING THE AD IN CITIES ALL OVER THE COUNTRY...
EVER SINCE THIS TRIAL BEGAN...
--BECAUSE BUCKY BARNES IS AN AMERICAN HERO. DON'T FORGET THAT.
Fred Davis, one-time "Bucky" stand-in

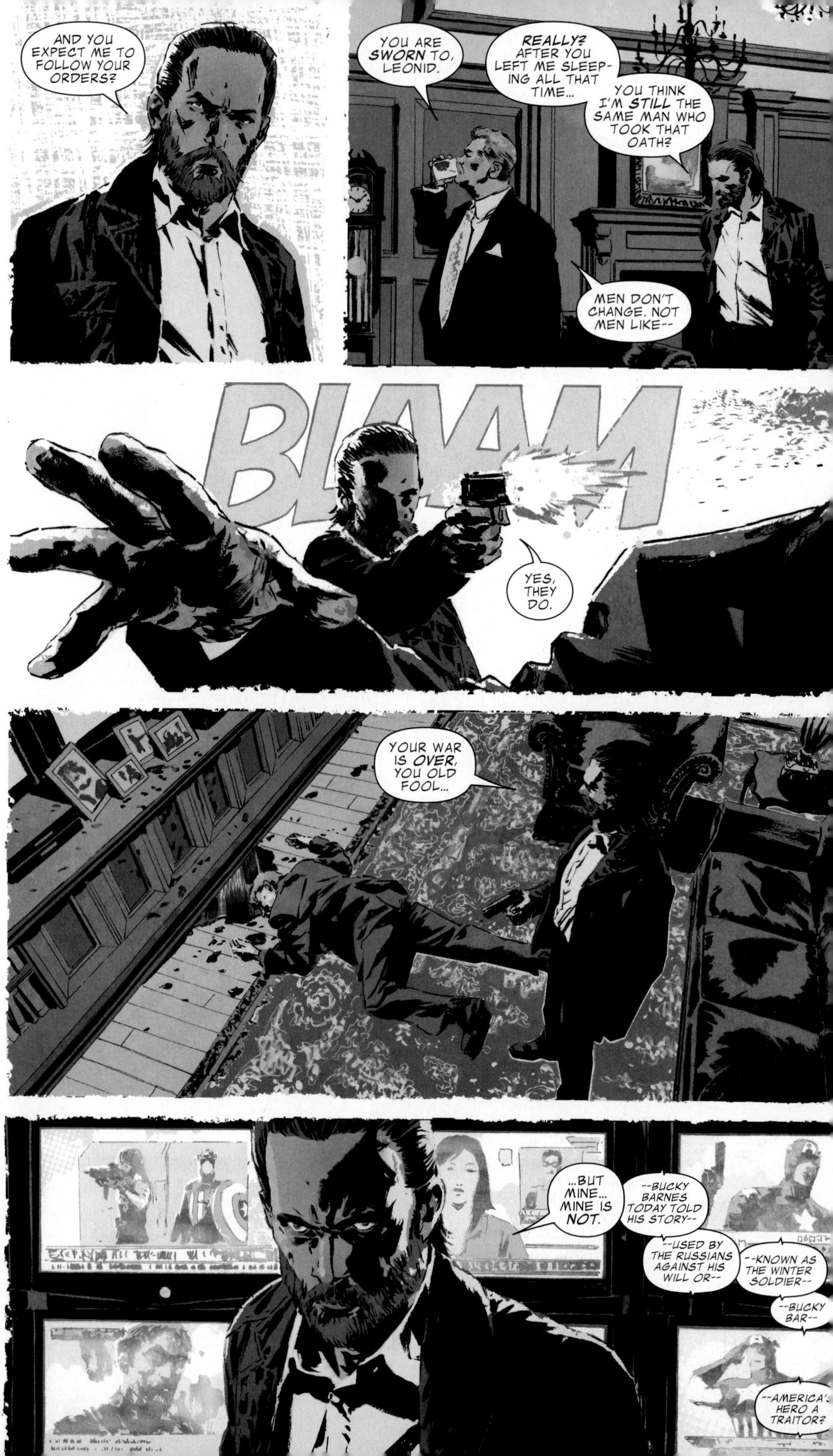

AND YOU EXPECT ME TO FOLLOW YOUR ORDERS?
YOU ARE **SWORN** TO, LEONID.
REALLY? AFTER YOU LEFT ME SLEEPING ALL THAT TIME...
YOU THINK I'M **STILL** THE SAME MAN WHO TOOK THAT OATH?
MEN DON'T CHANGE. NOT MEN LIKE--
BLAM
YES, THEY DO.
YOUR WAR IS **OVER**, YOU OLD FOOL...
...BUT MINE... MINE IS **NOT**.
--BUCKY BARNES TODAY TOLD HIS STORY--
--USED BY THE RUSSIANS AGAINST HIS WILL OR--
--KNOWN AS THE WINTER SOLDIER--
--BUCKY BAR--
--AMERICA'S HERO A TRAITOR?

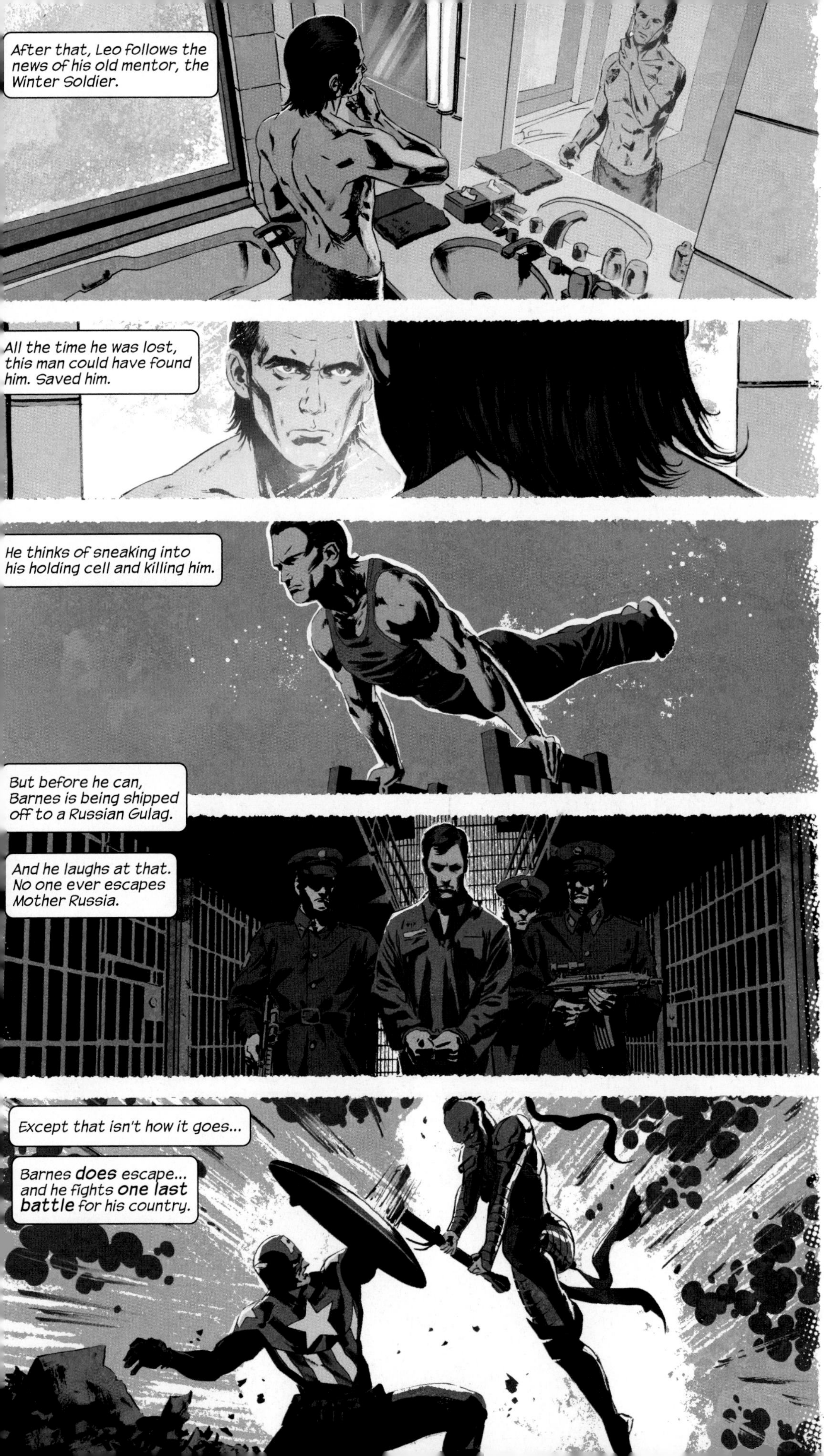
After that, Leo follows the news of his old mentor, the Winter Soldier.
All the time he was lost, this man could have found him. Saved him.
He thinks of sneaking into his holding cell and killing him.
But before he can, Barnes is being shipped off to a Russian Gulag.
And he laughs at that. No one ever escapes Mother Russia.
Except that isn't how it goes...
Barnes **does** escape... and he fights **one last battle** for his country.

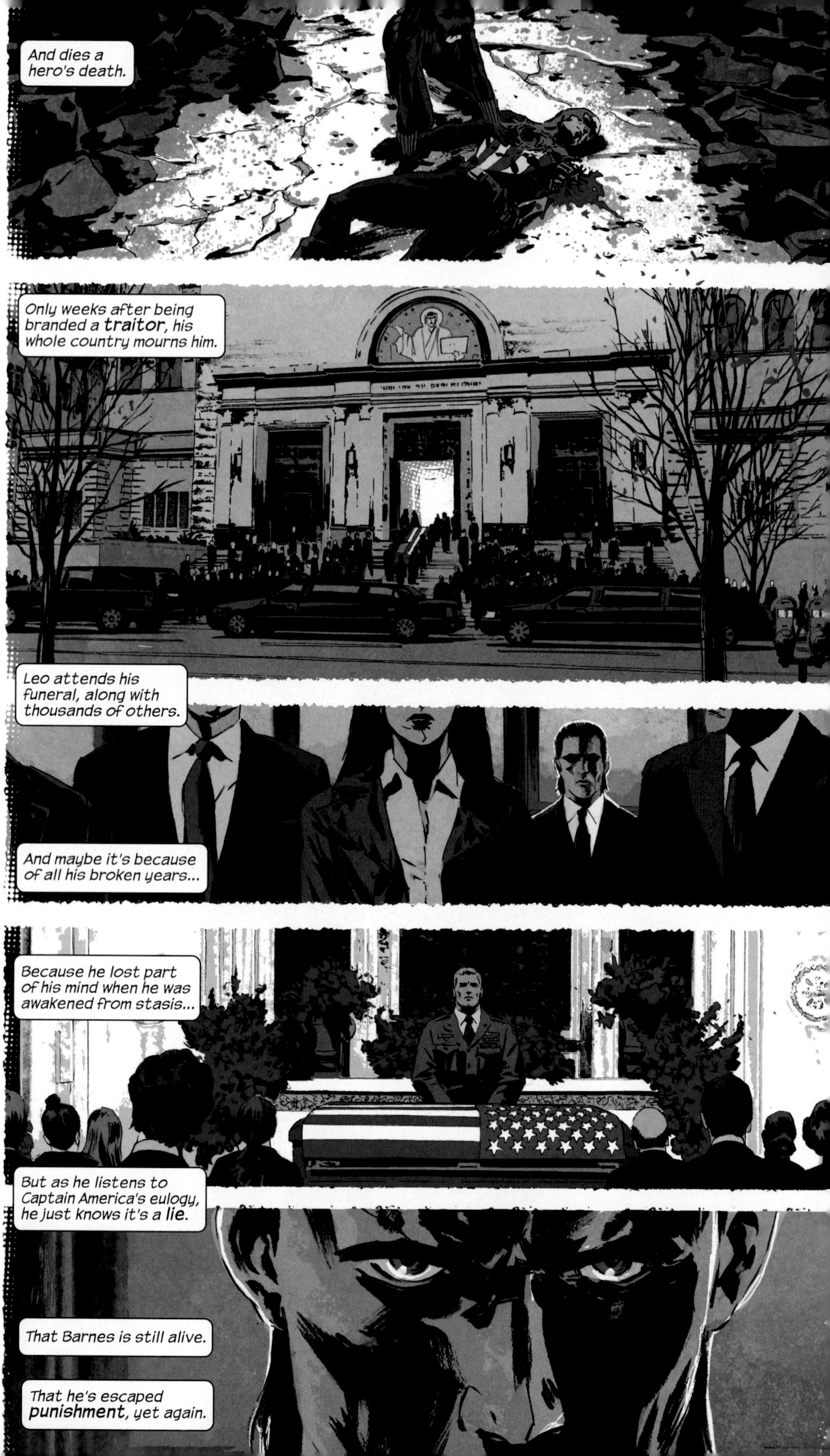
And dies a hero's death.
Only weeks after being branded a traitor, his whole country mourns him.
Leo attends his funeral, along with thousands of others.
And maybe it's because of all his broken years...
Because he lost part of his mind when he was awakened from stasis...
But as he listens to Captain America's eulogy, he just knows it's a lie.
That Barnes is still alive.
That he's escaped punishment, yet again.

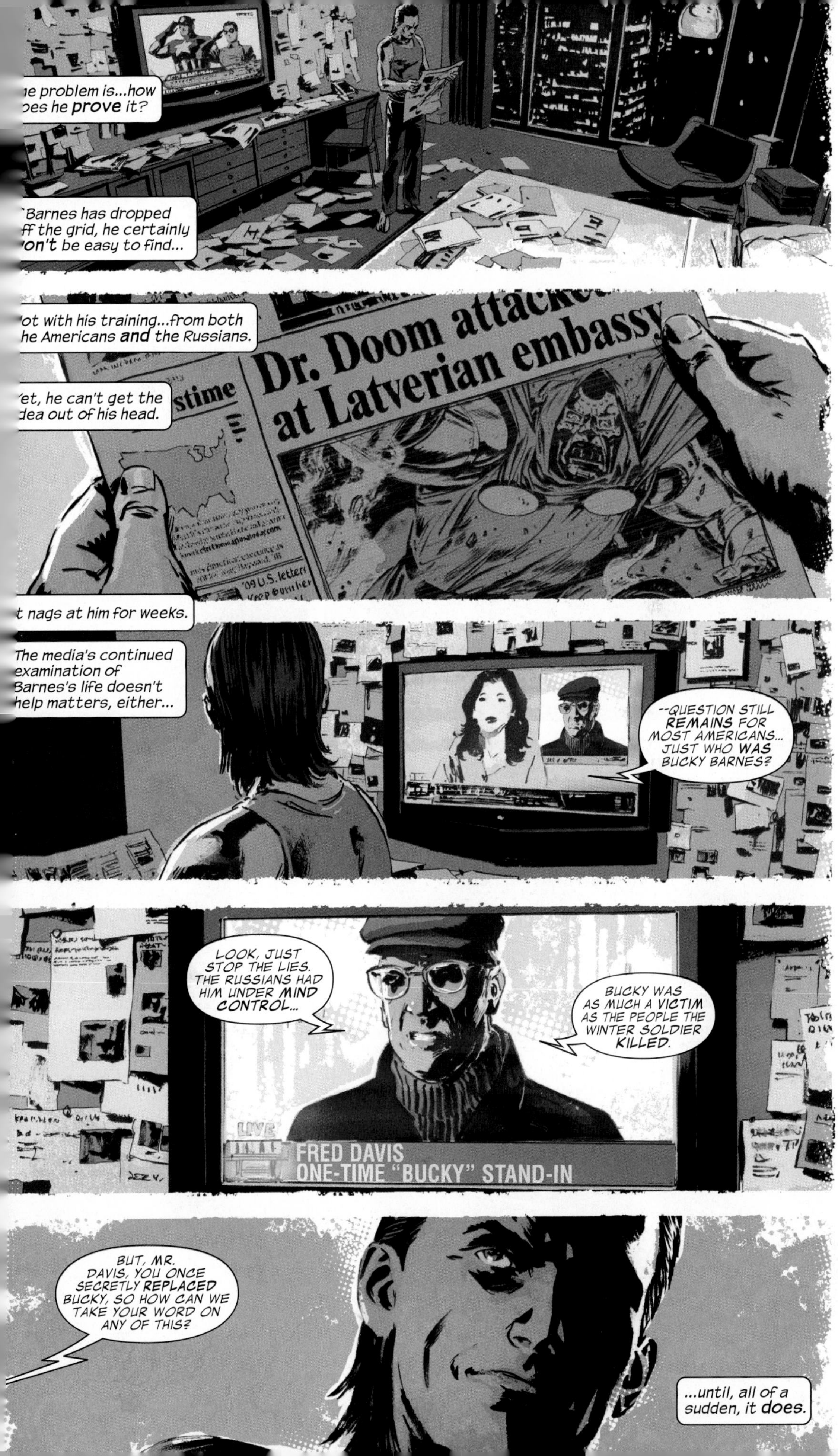

e problem is...how
oes he prove it?
Barnes has dropped
ff the grid, he certainly
on't be easy to find...
ot with his training...from both
he Americans and the Russians.
Dr. Doom attacke
at Latverian embassy
stime
'09 U.S. letters
et, he can't get the
dea out of his head.
t nags at him for weeks.
The media's continued examination of Barnes's life doesn't help matters, either...
--QUESTION STILL REMAINS FOR MOST AMERICANS... JUST WHO WAS BUCKY BARNES?
LOOK, JUST STOP THE LIES. THE RUSSIANS HAD HIM UNDER MIND CONTROL...
BUCKY WAS AS MUCH A VICTIM AS THE PEOPLE THE WINTER SOLDIER KILLED.
LIVE
FRED DAVIS
ONE-TIME "BUCKY" STAND-IN
BUT, MR. DAVIS, YOU ONCE SECRETLY REPLACED BUCKY, SO HOW CAN WE TAKE YOUR WORD ON ANY OF THIS?
...until, all of a sudden, it does.

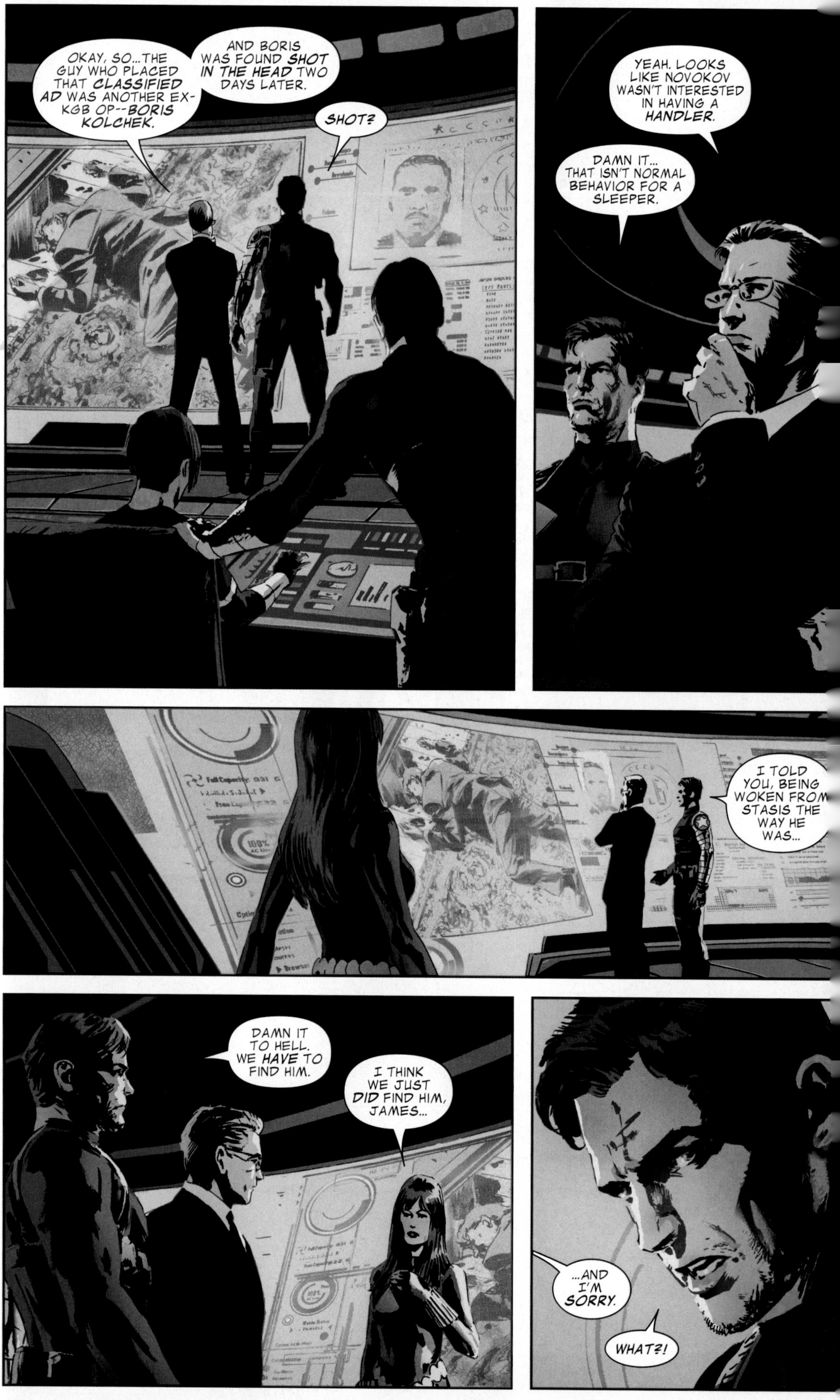

OKAY, SO...THE GUY WHO PLACED THAT CLASSIFIED AD WAS ANOTHER EX-KGB OP--BORIS KOLCHEK.
AND BORIS WAS FOUND SHOT IN THE HEAD TWO DAYS LATER.
SHOT?
YEAH. LOOKS LIKE NOVOKOV WASN'T INTERESTED IN HAVING A HANDLER.
DAMN IT... THAT ISN'T NORMAL BEHAVIOR FOR A SLEEPER.
I TOLD YOU, BEING WOKEN FROM STASIS THE WAY HE WAS...
DAMN IT TO HELL. WE HAVE TO FIND HIM.
I THINK WE JUST DID FIND HIM, JAMES...
...AND I'M SORRY.
WHAT?!

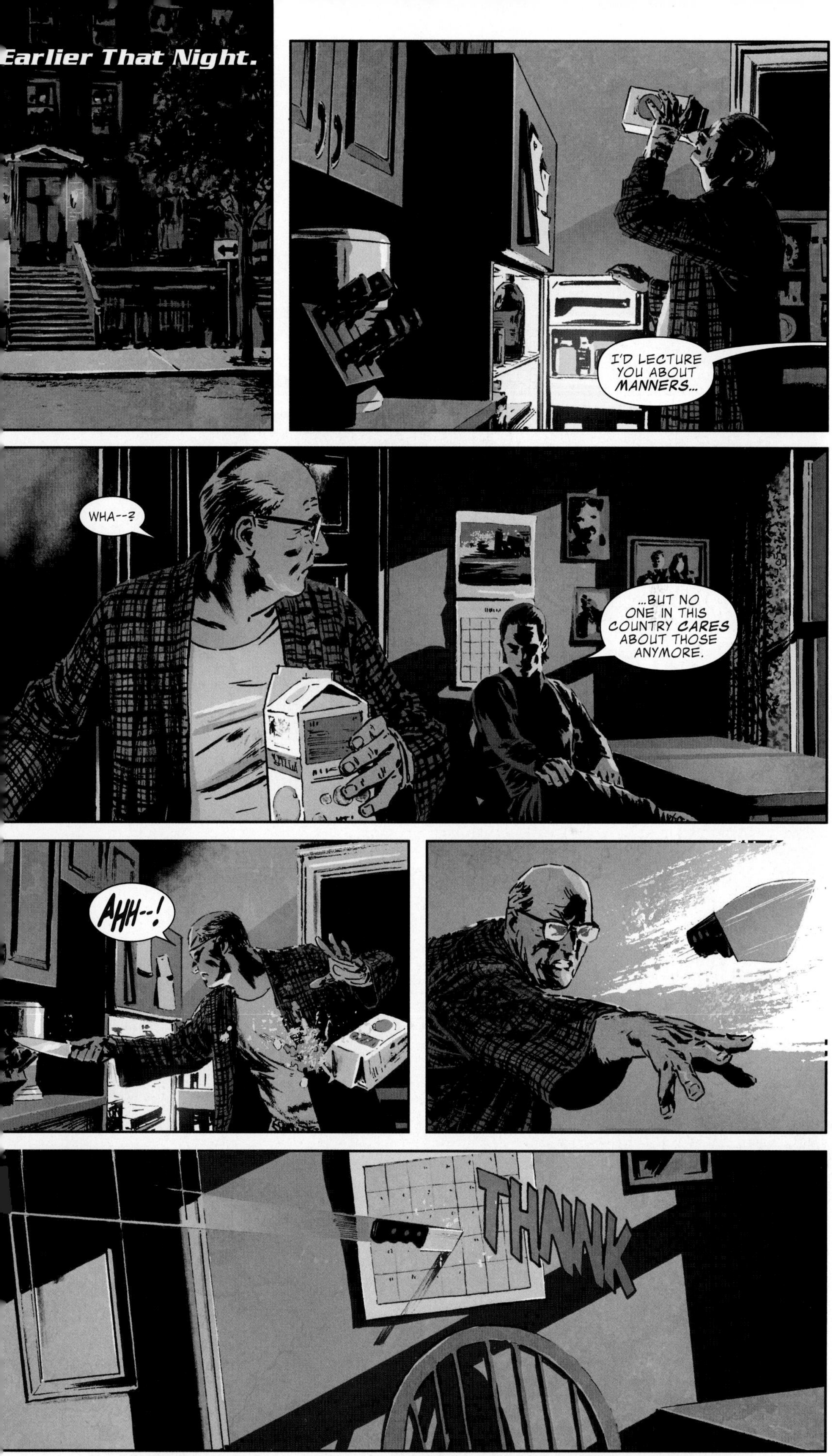
Earlier That Night.
I'D LECTURE YOU ABOUT MANNERS...
WHA--?
...BUT NO ONE IN THIS COUNTRY CARES ABOUT THOSE ANYMORE.
AHH--!
THNNK

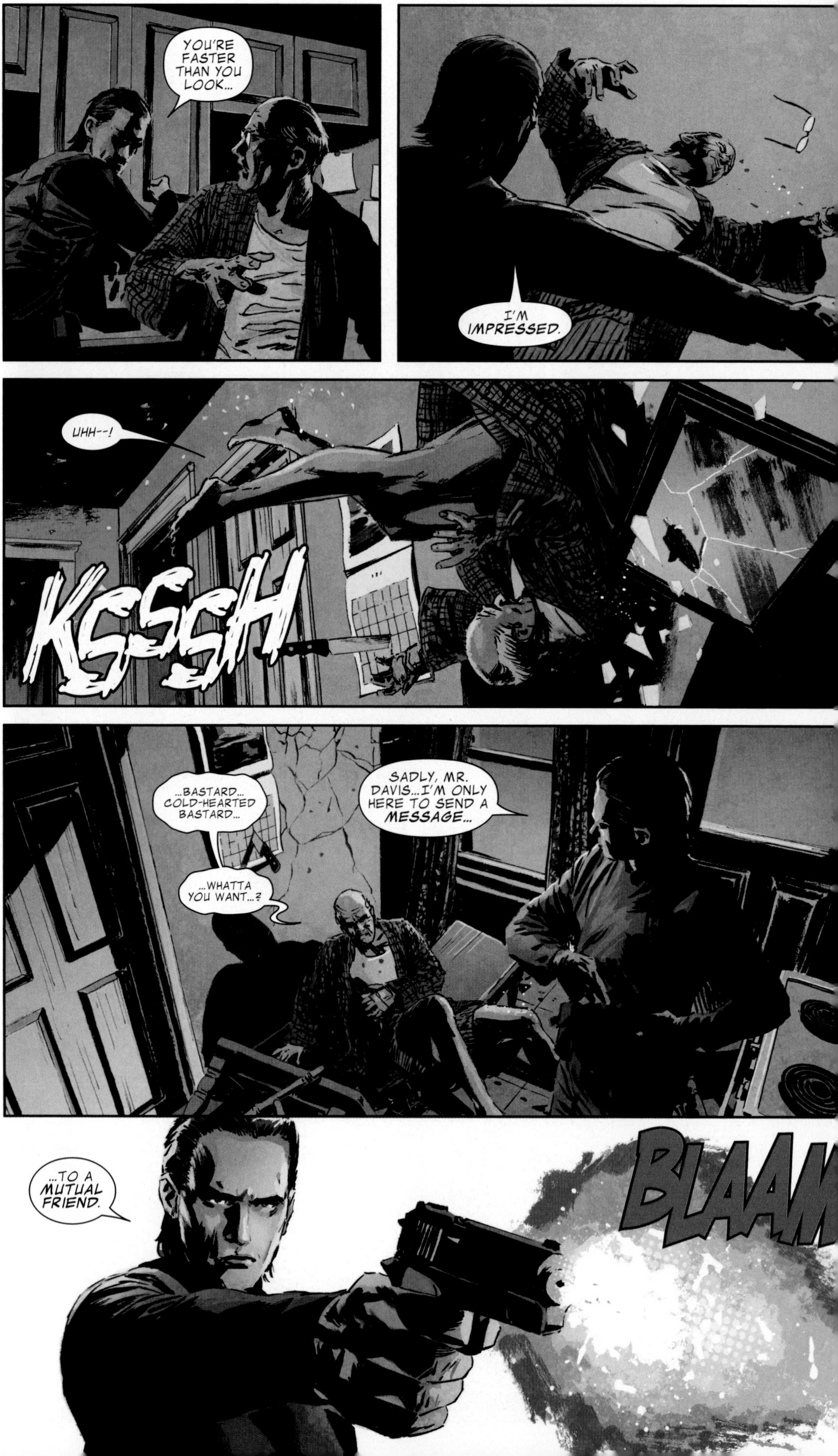
YOU'RE FASTER THAN YOU LOOK...
I'M IMPRESSED.
UHH--!
KSSSH
...BASTARD... COLD-HEARTED BASTARD...
SADLY, MR. DAVIS...I'M ONLY HERE TO SEND A MESSAGE...
...WHATTA YOU WANT...?
...TO A MUTUAL FRIEND.
BLAAM

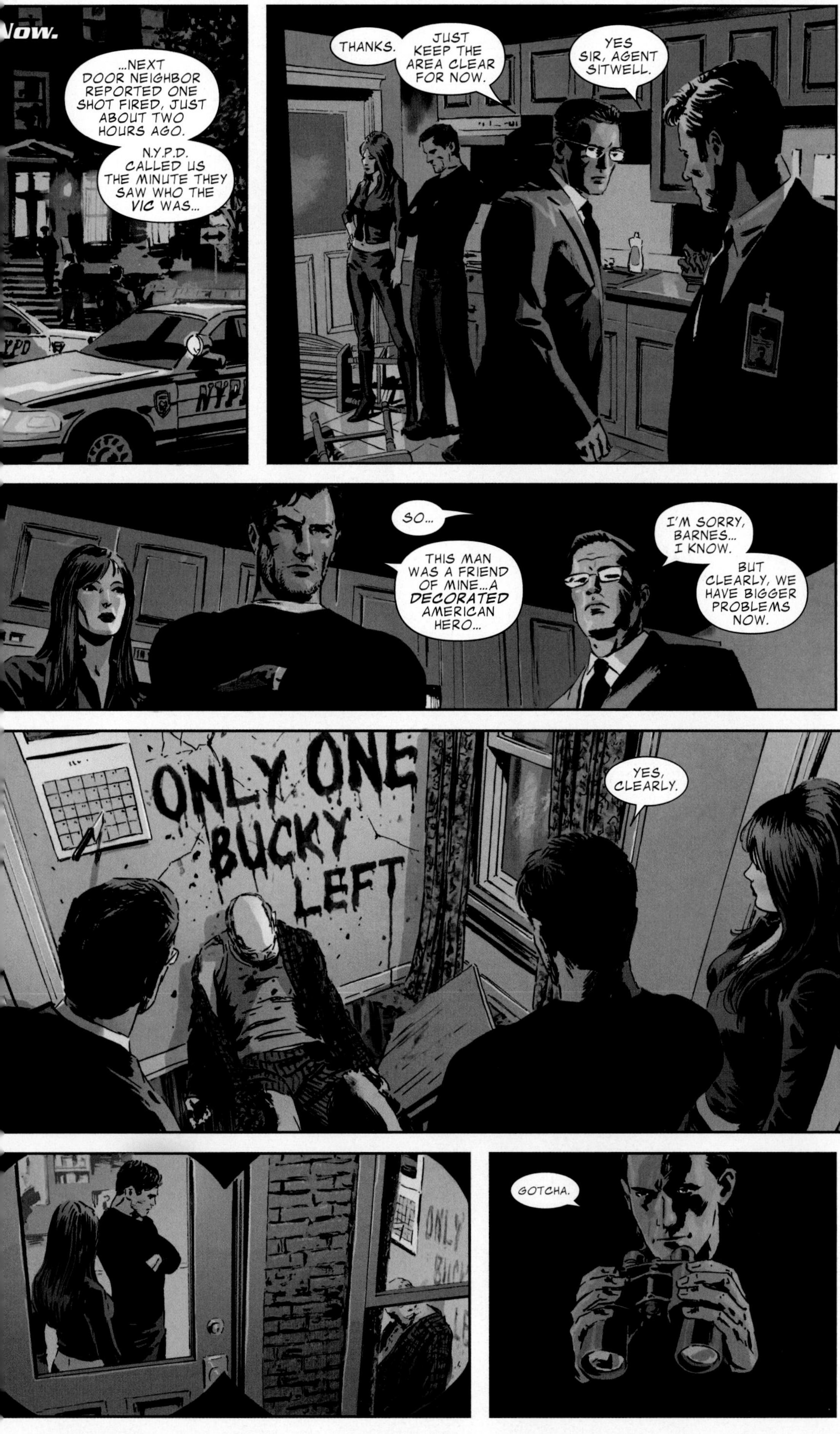
Now.
...NEXT DOOR NEIGHBOR REPORTED ONE SHOT FIRED, JUST ABOUT TWO HOURS AGO.
N.Y.P.D. CALLED US THE MINUTE THEY SAW WHO THE VIC WAS...
NYPD
THANKS.
JUST KEEP THE AREA CLEAR FOR NOW.
YES SIR, AGENT SITWELL.
SO...
THIS MAN WAS A FRIEND OF MINE...A DECORATED AMERICAN HERO...
I'M SORRY, BARNES... I KNOW.
BUT CLEARLY, WE HAVE BIGGER PROBLEMS NOW.
ONLY ONE BUCKY LEFT
YES, CLEARLY.
GOTCHA.

7

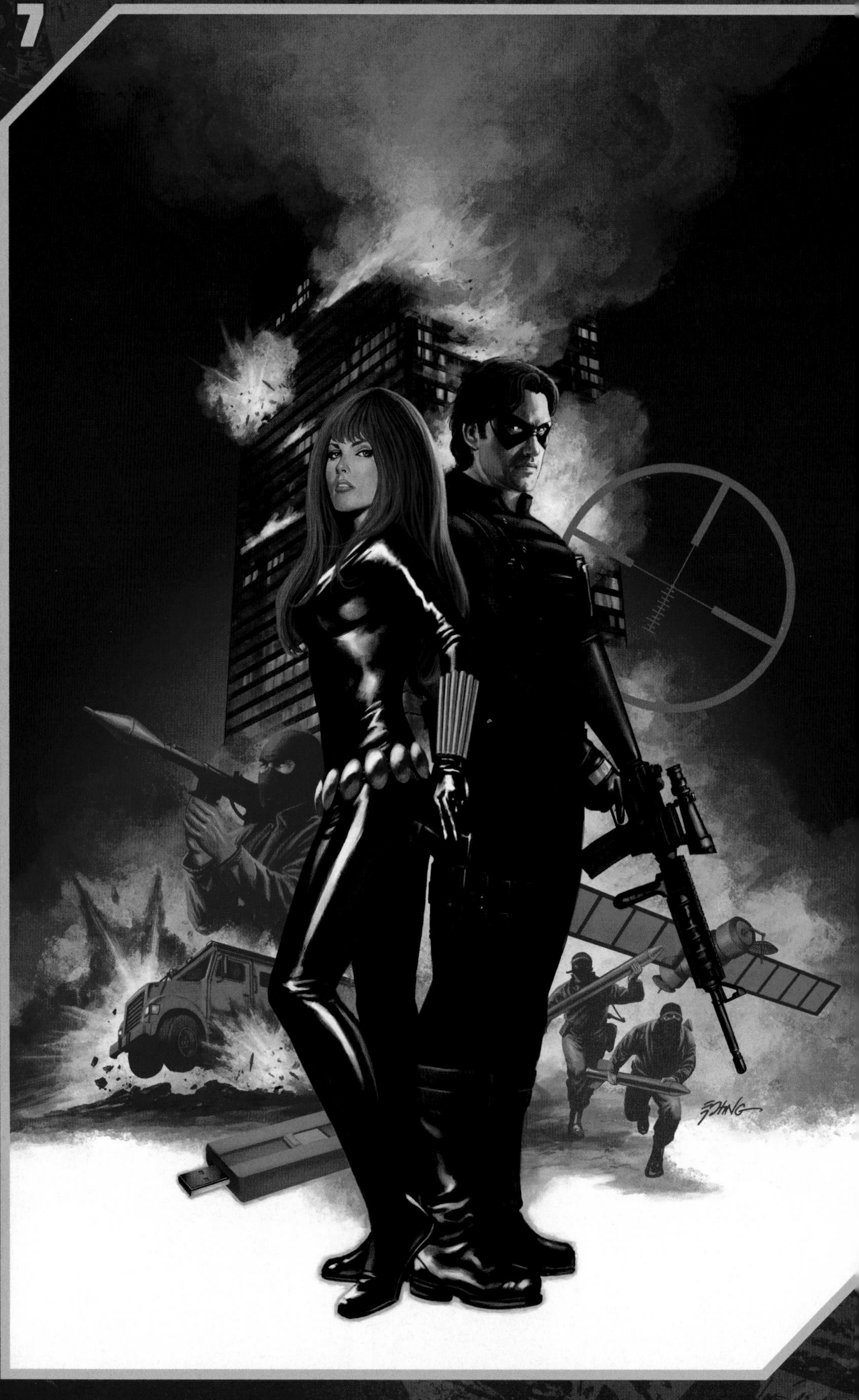

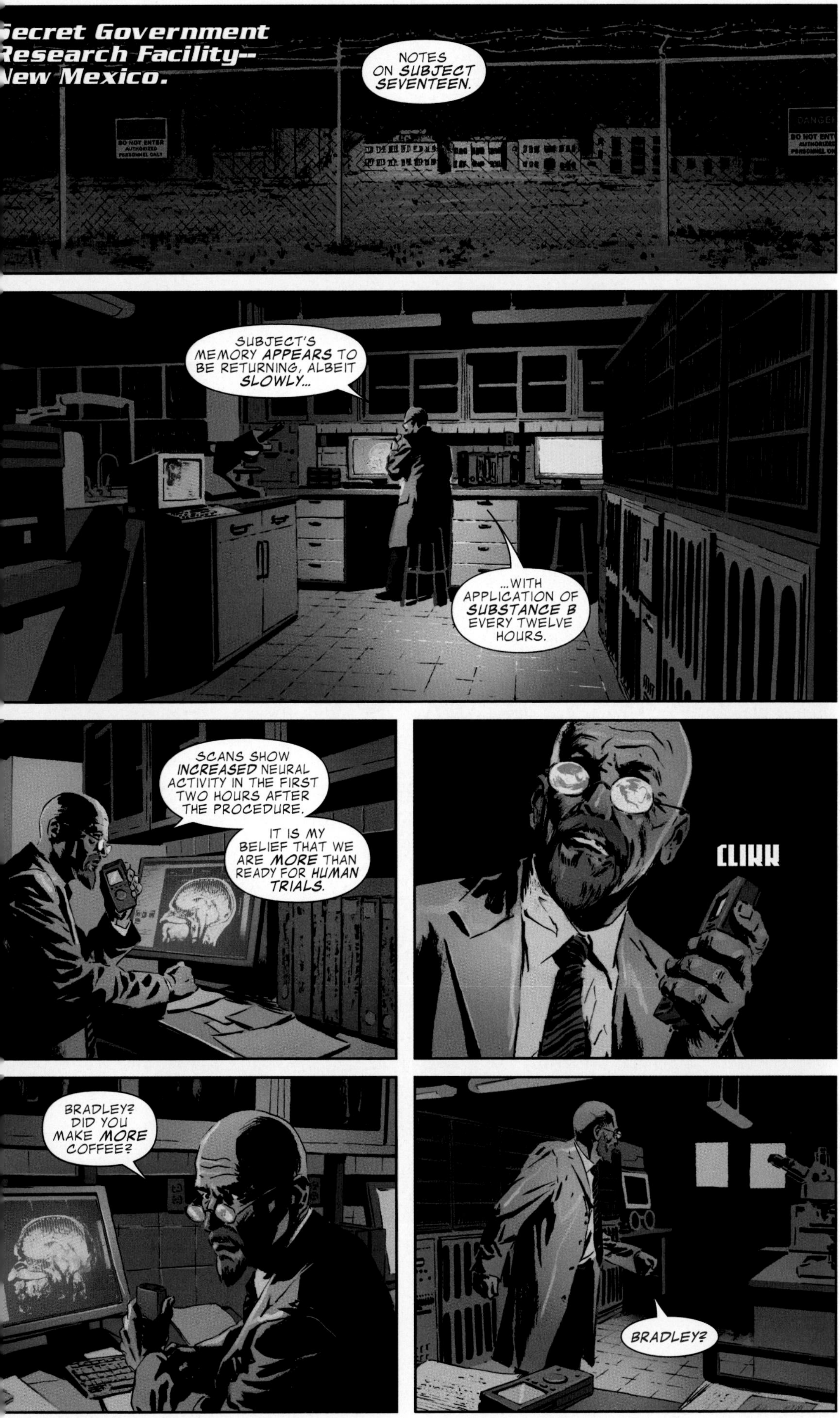
Secret Government Research Facility-- New Mexico.
NOTES ON SUBJECT SEVENTEEN.
DANGER DO NOT ENTER AUTHORIZED PERSONNEL ONLY
SUBJECT'S MEMORY APPEARS TO BE RETURNING, ALBEIT SLOWLY...
...WITH APPLICATION OF SUBSTANCE B EVERY TWELVE HOURS.
SCANS SHOW INCREASED NEURAL ACTIVITY IN THE FIRST TWO HOURS AFTER THE PROCEDURE.
IT IS MY BELIEF THAT WE ARE MORE THAN READY FOR HUMAN TRIALS.
CLIKK
BRADLEY? DID YOU MAKE MORE COFFEE?
BRADLEY?

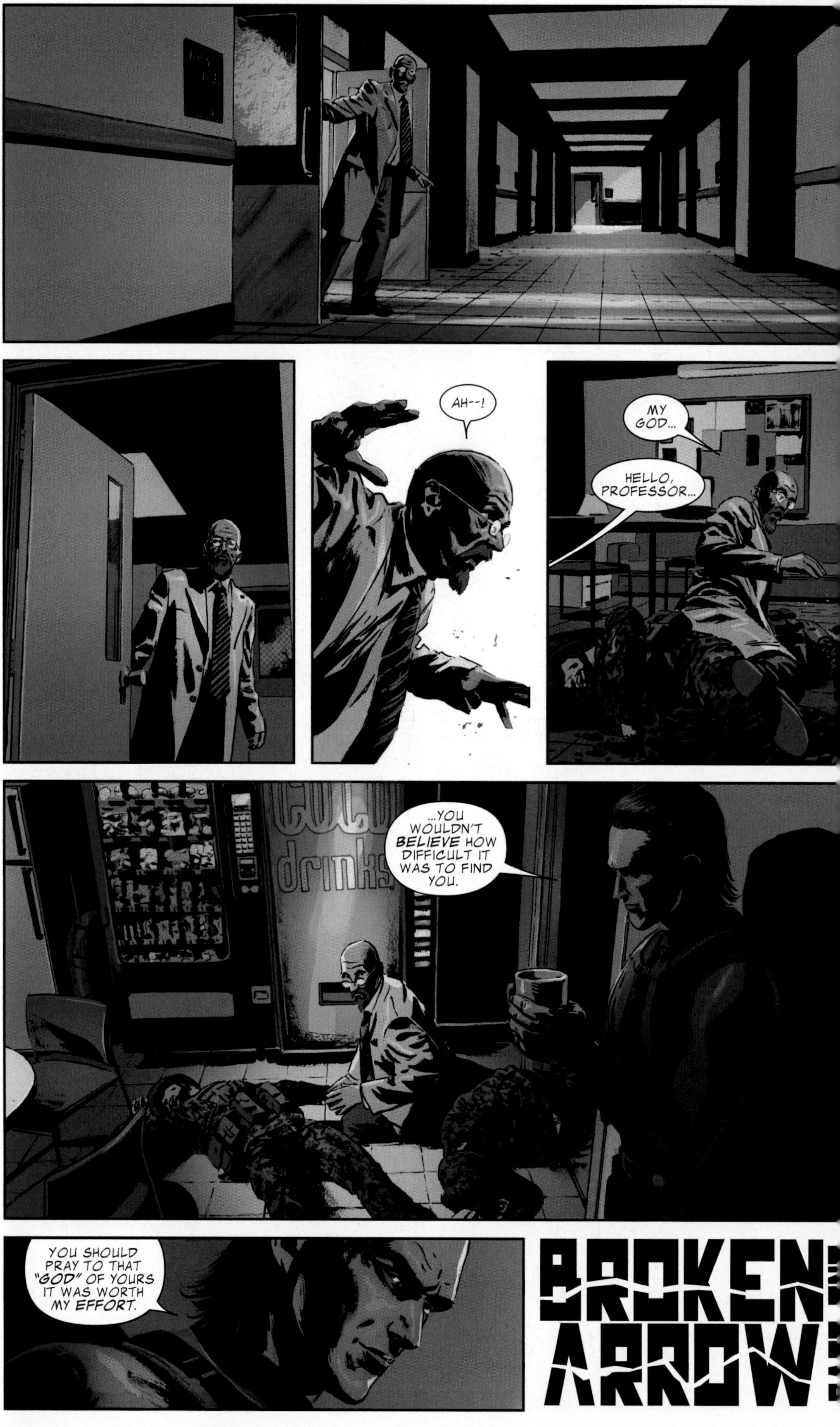
AH--!
MY GOD...
HELLO, PROFESSOR...
...YOU WOULDN'T BELIEVE HOW DIFFICULT IT WAS TO FIND YOU.
YOU SHOULD PRAY TO THAT "GOD" OF YOURS IT WAS WORTH MY EFFORT.
BROKEN ARROW

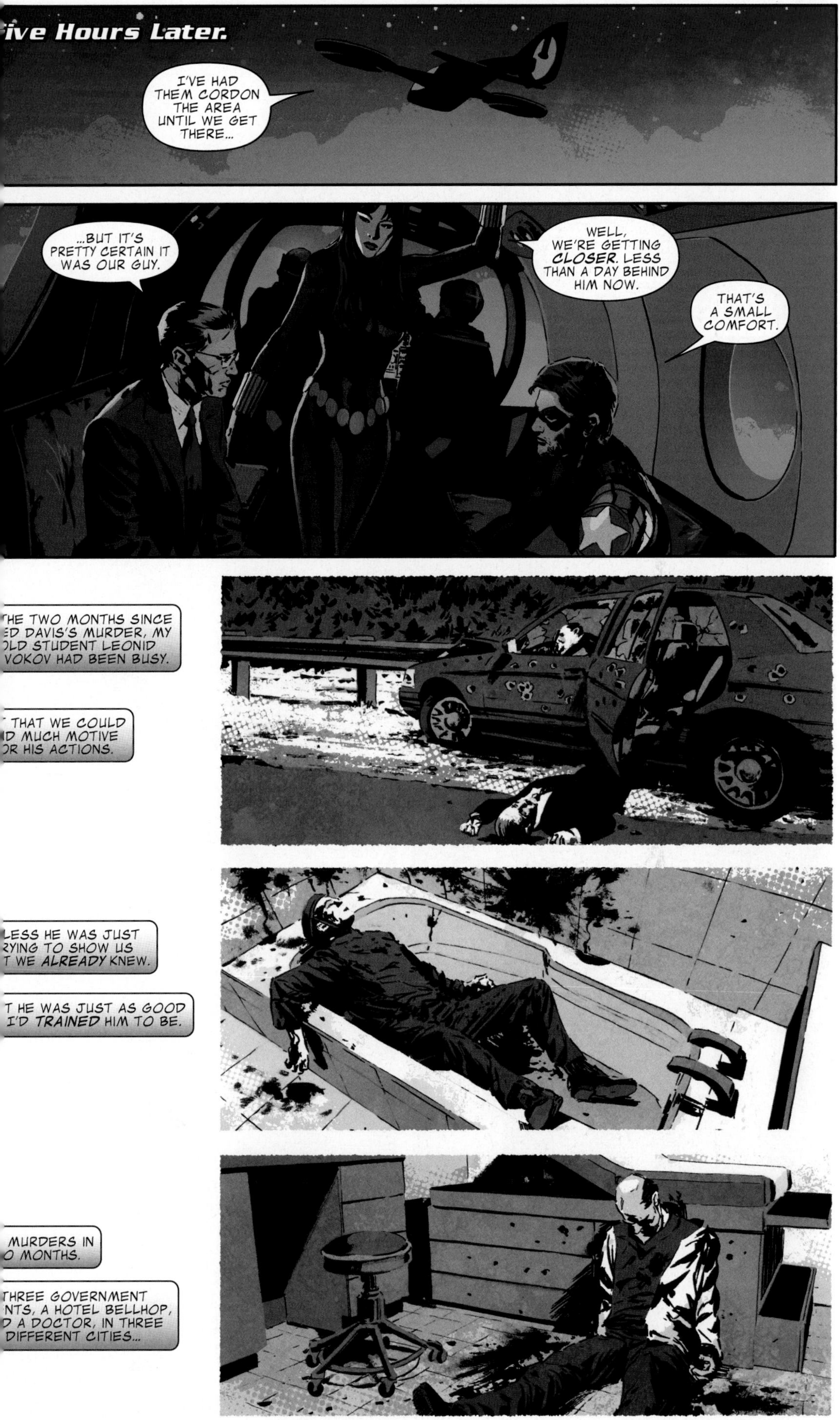

ive Hours Later.
I'VE HAD THEM CORDON THE AREA UNTIL WE GET THERE...
...BUT IT'S PRETTY CERTAIN IT WAS OUR GUY.
WELL, WE'RE GETTING CLOSER. LESS THAN A DAY BEHIND HIM NOW.
THAT'S A SMALL COMFORT.
HE TWO MONTHS SINCE ED DAVIS'S MURDER, MY LD STUDENT LEONID VOKOV HAD BEEN BUSY.
THAT WE COULD D MUCH MOTIVE R HIS ACTIONS.
LESS HE WAS JUST RYING TO SHOW US T WE ALREADY KNEW.
T HE WAS JUST AS GOOD I'D TRAINED HIM TO BE.
MURDERS IN O MONTHS.
THREE GOVERNMENT NTS, A HOTEL BELLHOP, D A DOCTOR, IN THREE DIFFERENT CITIES...

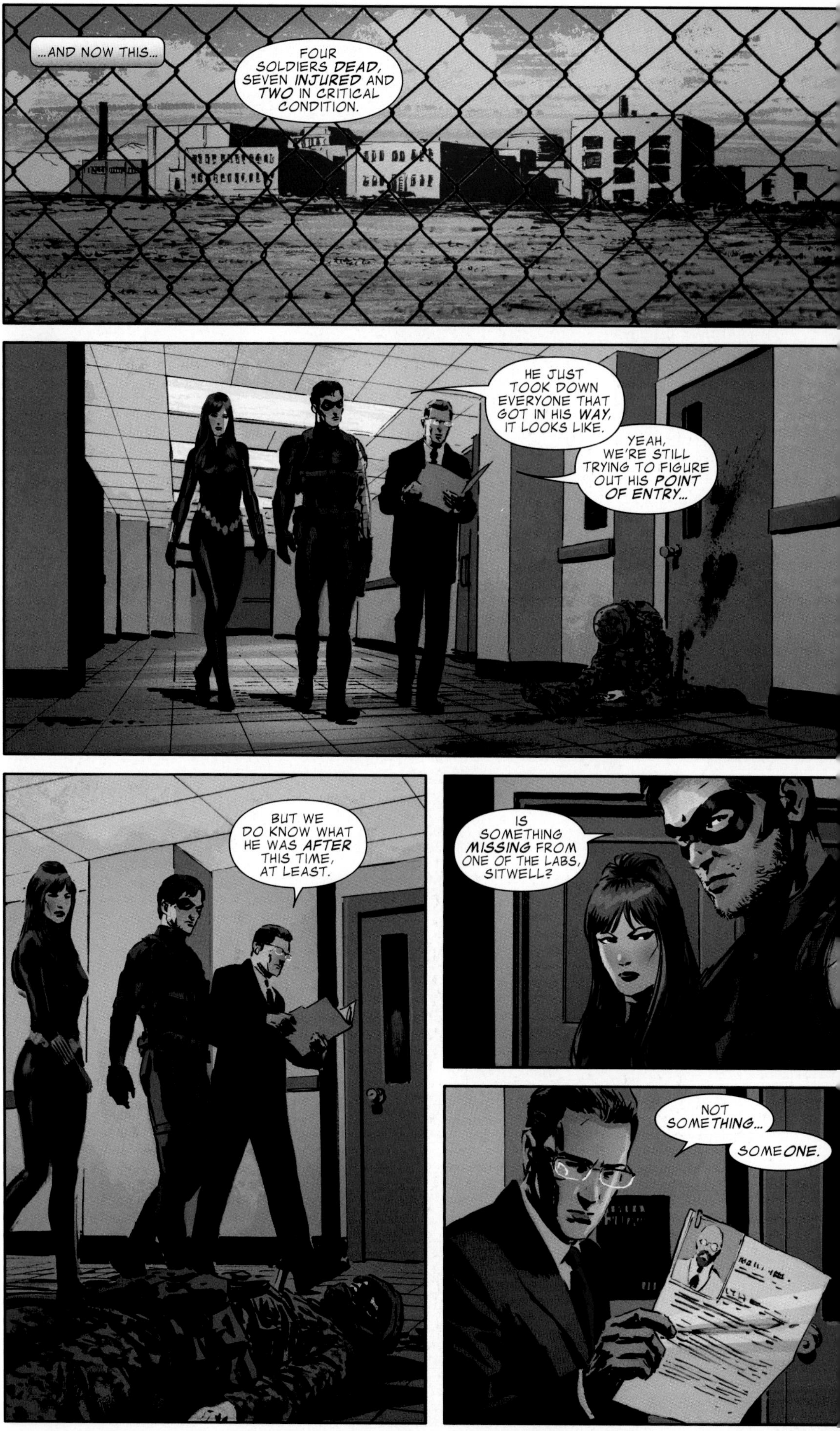
...AND NOW THIS...
FOUR SOLDIERS DEAD, SEVEN INJURED AND TWO IN CRITICAL CONDITION.
HE JUST TOOK DOWN EVERYONE THAT GOT IN HIS WAY, IT LOOKS LIKE.
YEAH, WE'RE STILL TRYING TO FIGURE OUT HIS POINT OF ENTRY...
BUT WE DO KNOW WHAT HE WAS AFTER THIS TIME, AT LEAST.
IS SOMETHING MISSING FROM ONE OF THE LABS, SITWELL?
NOT SOMETHING...
SOMEONE.

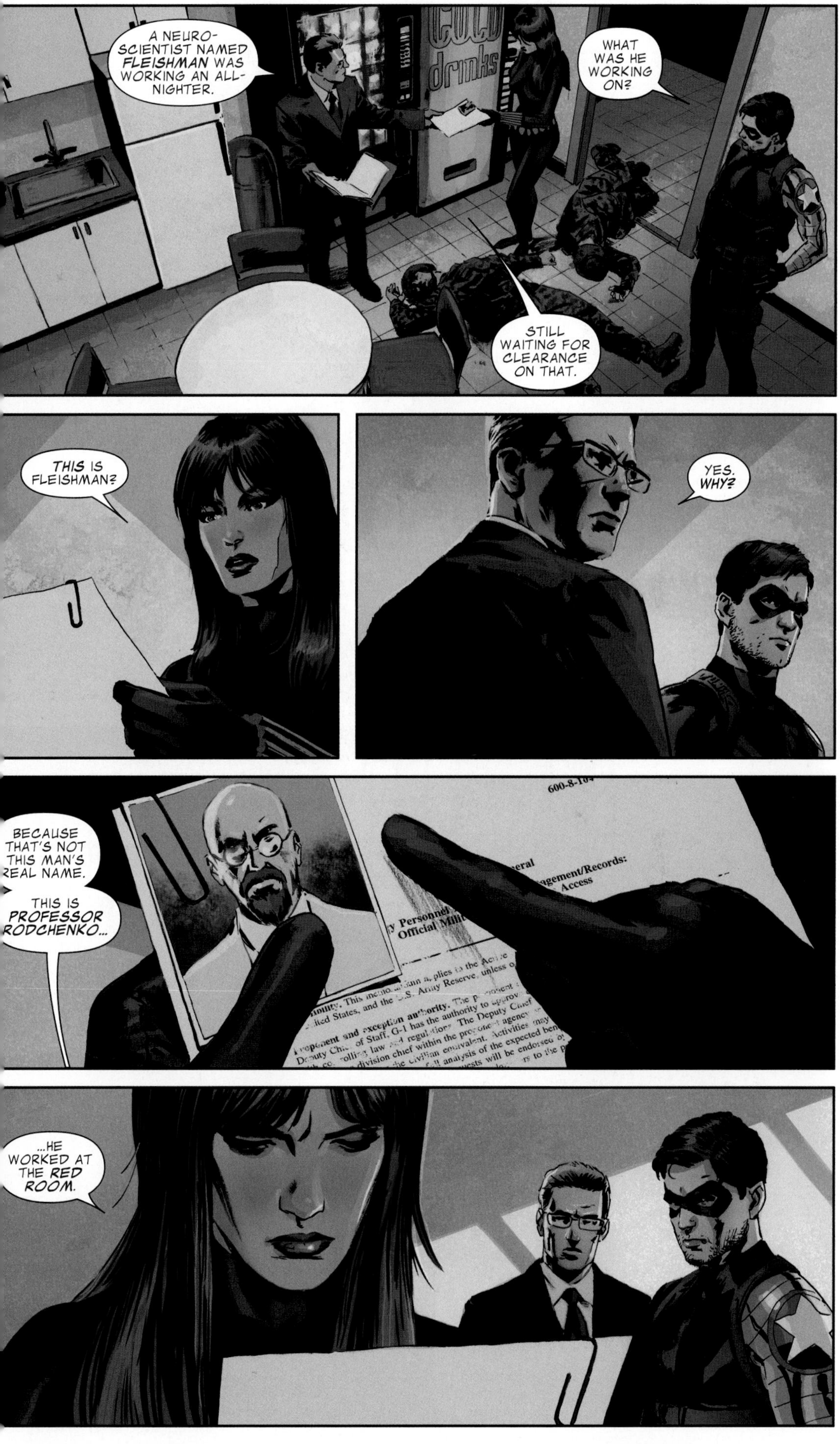
A NEURO-SCIENTIST NAMED FLEISHMAN WAS WORKING AN ALL-NIGHTER.
WHAT WAS HE WORKING ON?
STILL WAITING FOR CLEARANCE ON THAT.
THIS IS FLEISHMAN?
YES. WHY?
BECAUSE THAT'S NOT THIS MAN'S REAL NAME.
THIS IS PROFESSOR RODCHENKO...
...HE WORKED AT THE RED ROOM.

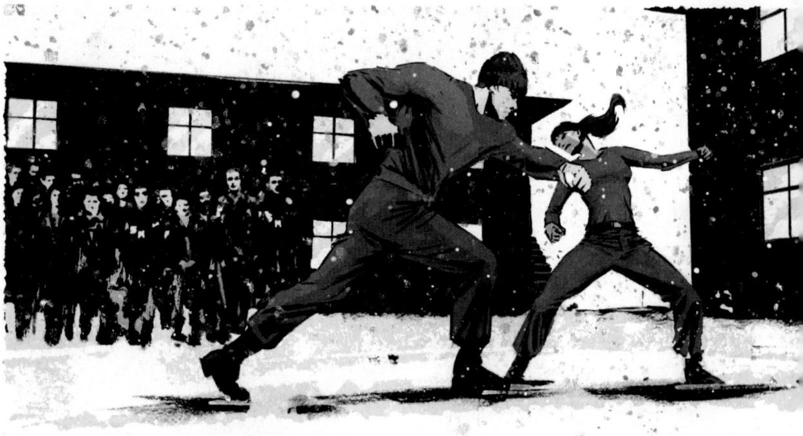

FROM THE EARLY 1950S THROUGH THE FALL OF THE SOVIET UNION, THE ***RED ROOM*** WAS A ***TRAINING PROGRAM*** IN MOSCOW.

ONE OF THE MANY ARMS OF ***DEPARTMENT X***, THE KGB'S EXPERIMENTAL SCIENCE DIVISION.

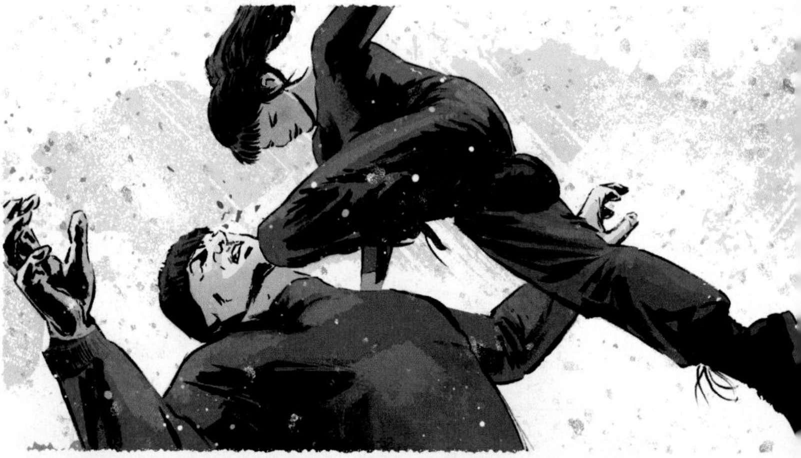

IT'S WHERE NATASHA WAS RAISED...

WHERE SHE EARNED THE RANK OF BLACK WIDOW...

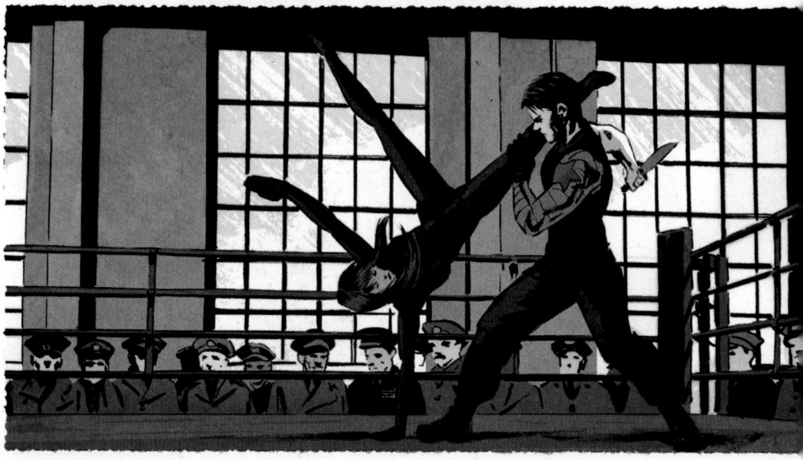

AND WHERE, IN THE LATE 1950S, SHE MET ***ME***.

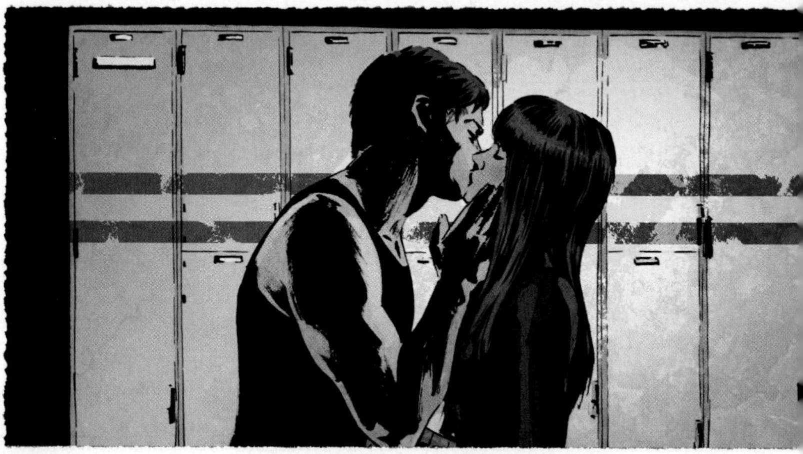

BACK WHEN NEITHER SHE ***NOR*** I KNEW EXACTLY ***WHO*** I WAS.

ONE OF
DEPARTMENT X'S
SPECIALTIES WAS
BRAINWASHING.

ERASING MEMORIES,
IMPLANTING NEW ONES,
EVEN TURNING MEN
INTO PREPROGRAMMED
SLAVES.

THEY EXPERIMENTED
WITH ALL KINDS OF
TECHNIQUES, TOO.

HALLUCINOGENS,
MICROCHIPS, SENSORY
DEPRIVATION.

WHATEVER KIND OF
TORTURE THEY FELT
WAS NECESSARY.

THESE EXPERIENCES
ARE ONE OF THE
THINGS NATASHA AND
I HAVE IN COMMON.

WE'VE BOTH HAD OUR
HEADS MESSED WITH
WAY TOO OFTEN.

RODCHENKO
WAS ONE OF THE
RED ROOM'S MAIN
PROGRAMMERS IN
THE MID-1970S...

HE
IMPLANTED
COVER IDENTITIES
INTO OPERATIVES
PRE-MISSION.

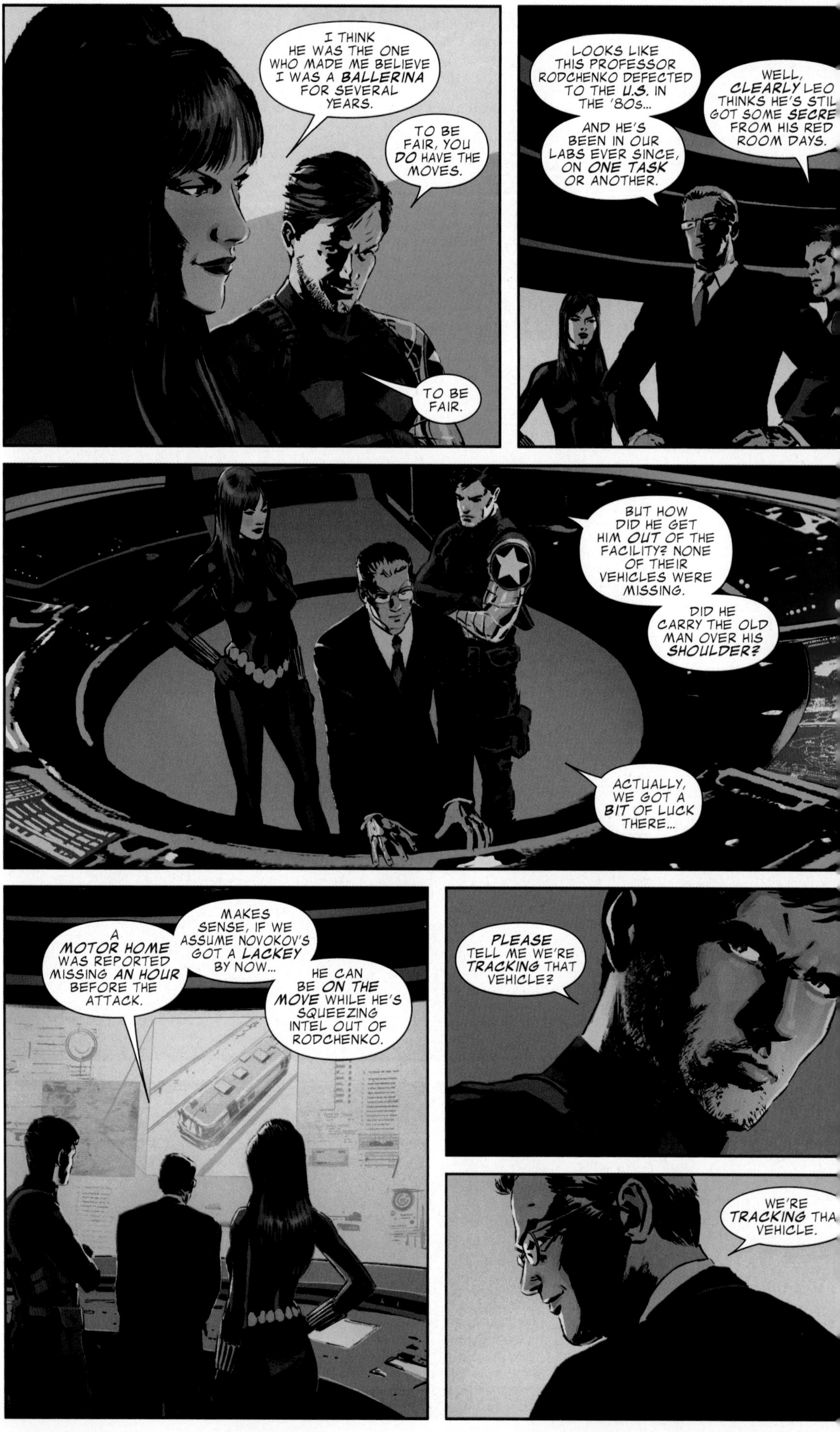
I THINK HE WAS THE ONE WHO MADE ME BELIEVE I WAS A BALLERINA FOR SEVERAL YEARS.
TO BE FAIR, YOU DO HAVE THE MOVES.
TO BE FAIR.
LOOKS LIKE THIS PROFESSOR RODCHENKO DEFECTED TO THE U.S. IN THE '80s...
AND HE'S BEEN IN OUR LABS EVER SINCE, ON ONE TASK OR ANOTHER.
WELL, CLEARLY LEO THINKS HE'S STIL GOT SOME SECRE FROM HIS RED ROOM DAYS.
BUT HOW DID HE GET HIM OUT OF THE FACILITY? NONE OF THEIR VEHICLES WERE MISSING.
DID HE CARRY THE OLD MAN OVER HIS SHOULDER?
ACTUALLY, WE GOT A BIT OF LUCK THERE...
A MOTOR HOME WAS REPORTED MISSING AN HOUR BEFORE THE ATTACK.
MAKES SENSE, IF WE ASSUME NOVOKOV'S GOT A LACKEY BY NOW...
HE CAN BE ON THE MOVE WHILE HE'S SQUEEZING INTEL OUT OF RODCHENKO.
PLEASE TELL ME WE'RE TRACKING THAT VEHICLE?
WE'RE TRACKING THA VEHICLE.

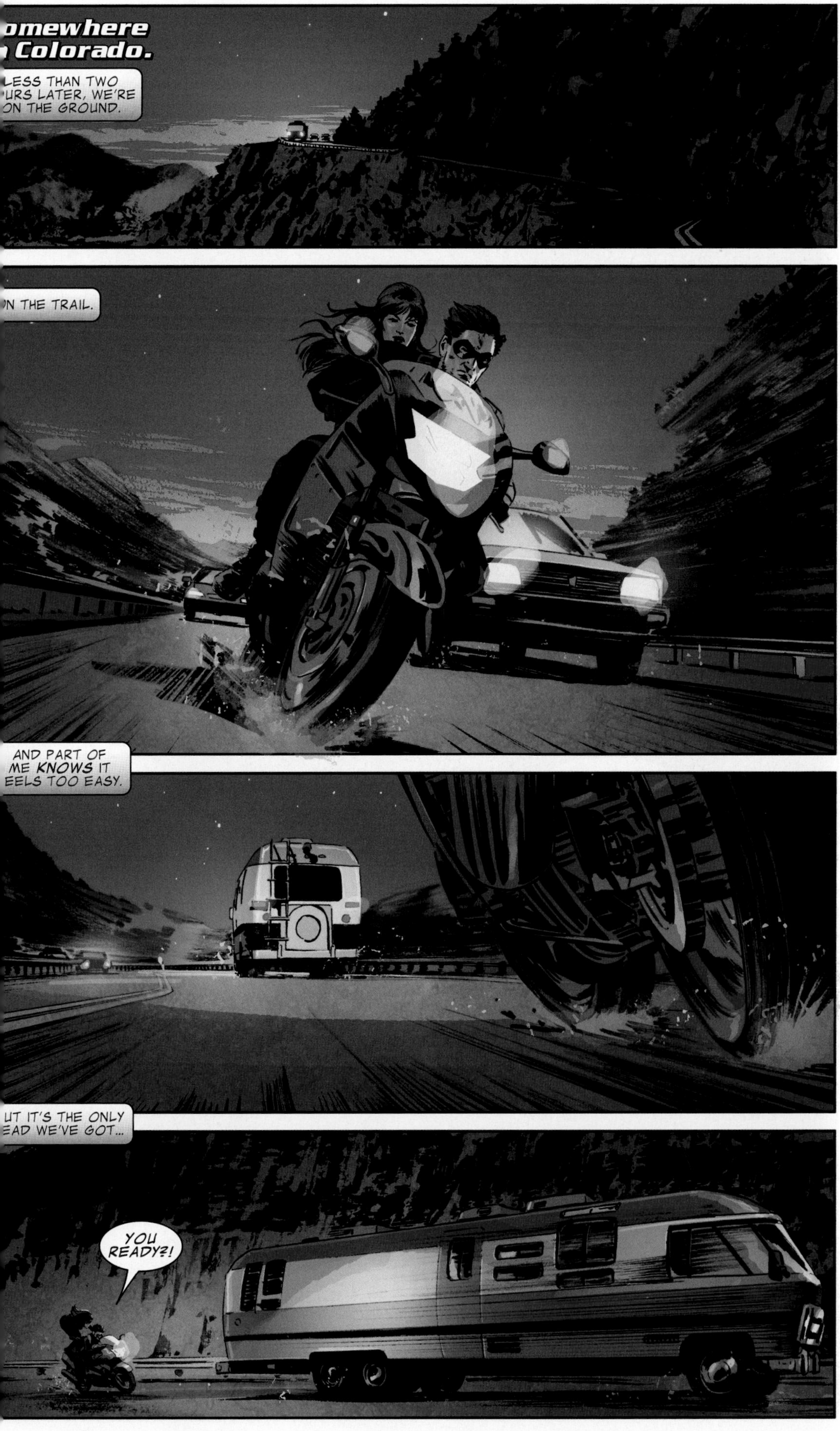

omewhere
Colorado.
LESS THAN TWO URS LATER, WE'RE ON THE GROUND.
N THE TRAIL.
AND PART OF ME KNOWS IT EELS TOO EASY.
UT IT'S THE ONLY EAD WE'VE GOT...
YOU READY?!

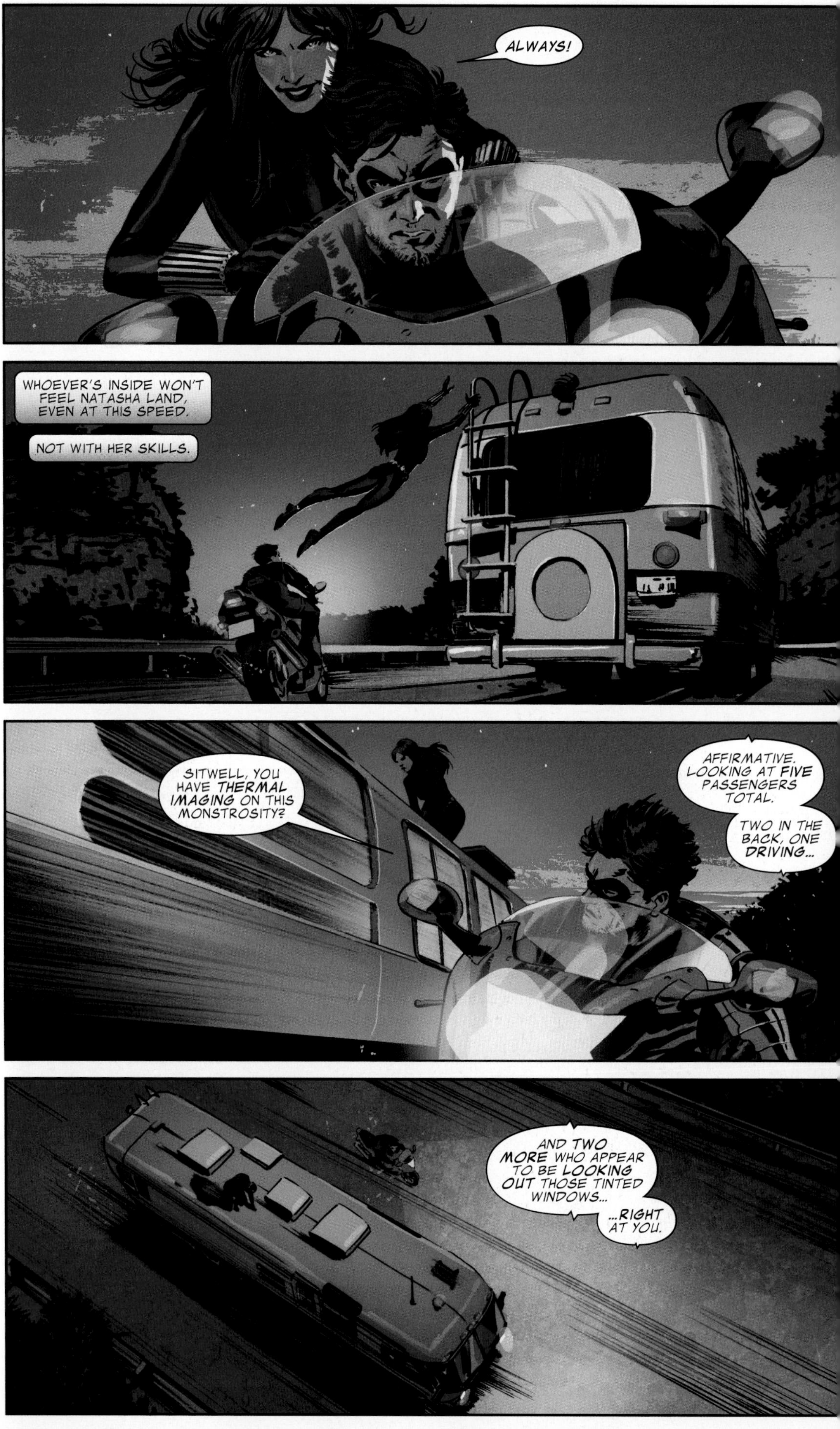
ALWAYS!
WHOEVER'S INSIDE WON'T FEEL NATASHA LAND, EVEN AT THIS SPEED.
NOT WITH HER SKILLS.
SITWELL, YOU HAVE THERMAL IMAGING ON THIS MONSTROSITY?
AFFIRMATIVE. LOOKING AT FIVE PASSENGERS TOTAL.
TWO IN THE BACK, ONE DRIVING...
AND TWO MORE WHO APPEAR TO BE LOOKING OUT THOSE TINTED WINDOWS...
...RIGHT AT YOU.

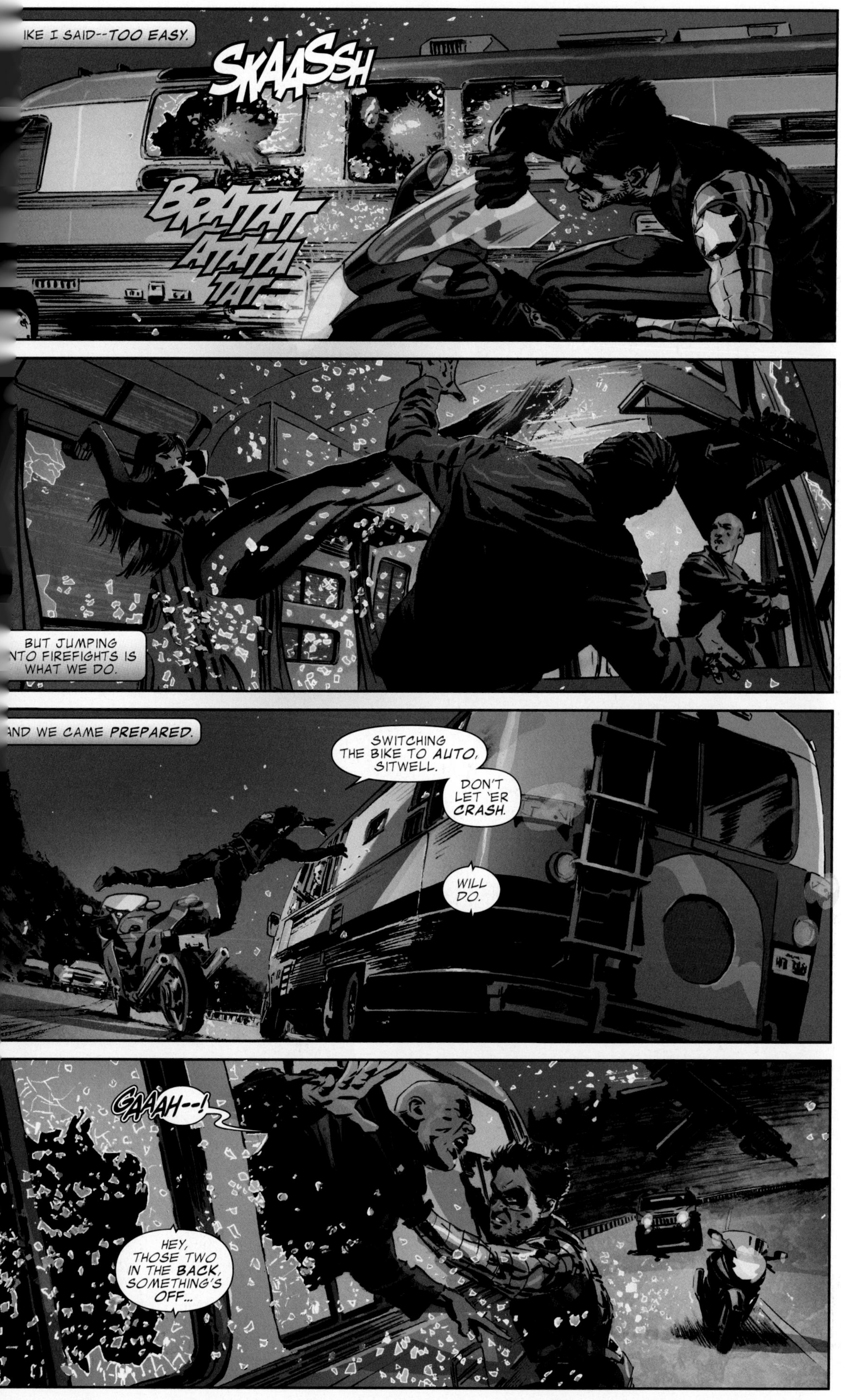
IKE I SAID--TOO EASY.
SKAASSH
BRATATATATATATAT--
BUT JUMPING
NTO FIREFIGHTS IS
WHAT WE DO.
AND WE CAME PREPARED.
SWITCHING THE BIKE TO AUTO, SITWELL.
DON'T LET 'ER CRASH.
WILL DO.
GAAAH--!
HEY, THOSE TWO IN THE BACK, SOMETHING'S OFF...

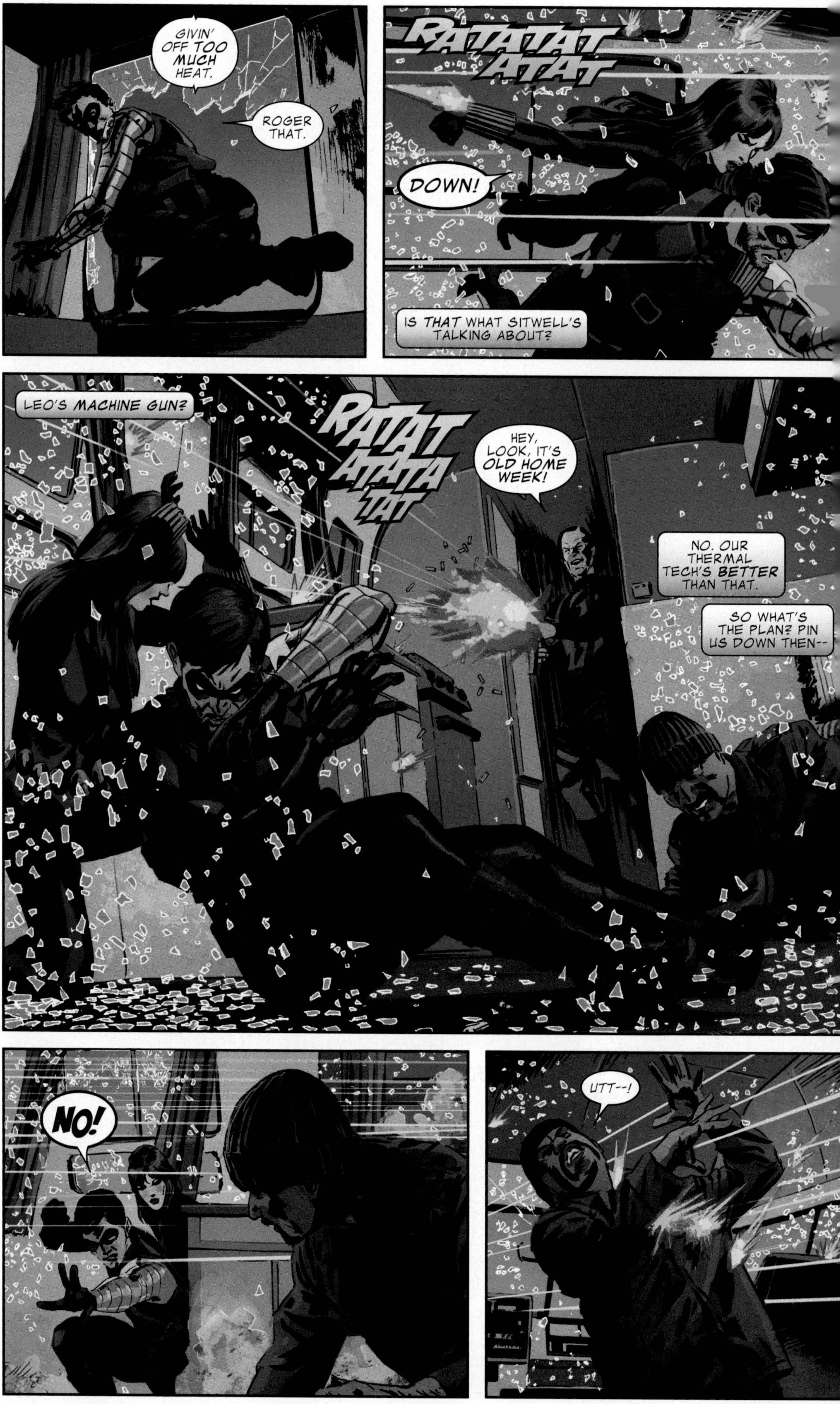
GIVIN' OFF TOO MUCH HEAT.
ROGER THAT.
RATATAT ATAT
DOWN!
IS THAT WHAT SITWELL'S TALKING ABOUT?
LEO'S MACHINE GUN?
RATATAT ATATA TAT
HEY, LOOK, IT'S OLD HOME WEEK!
NO. OUR THERMAL TECH'S BETTER THAN THAT.
SO WHAT'S THE PLAN? PIN US DOWN THEN--
NO!
UTT--!

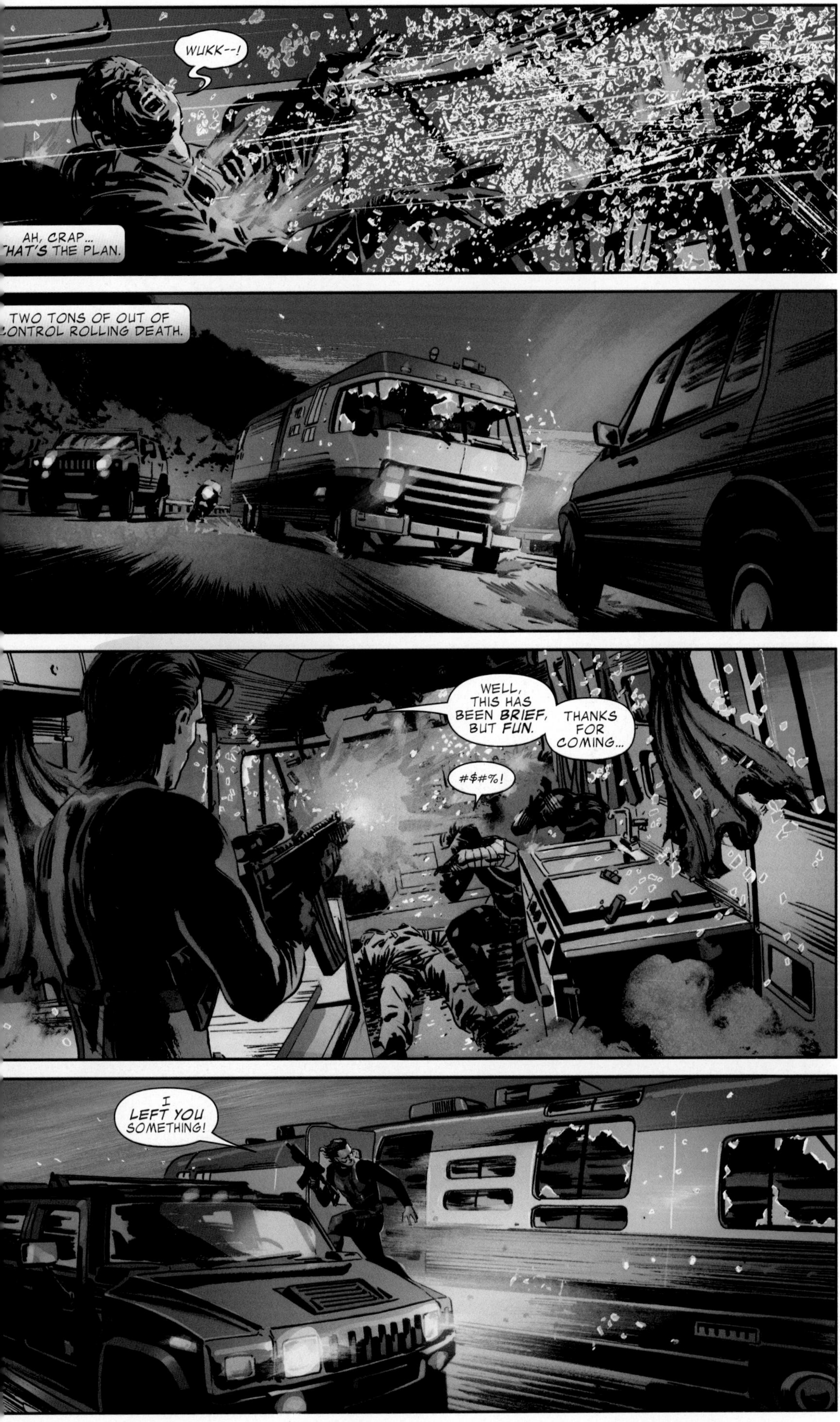
WUKK--!
AH, CRAP... THAT'S THE PLAN.
TWO TONS OF OUT OF CONTROL ROLLING DEATH.
WELL, THIS HAS BEEN BRIEF, BUT FUN.
THANKS FOR COMING...
#$#%!
I LEFT YOU SOMETHING!

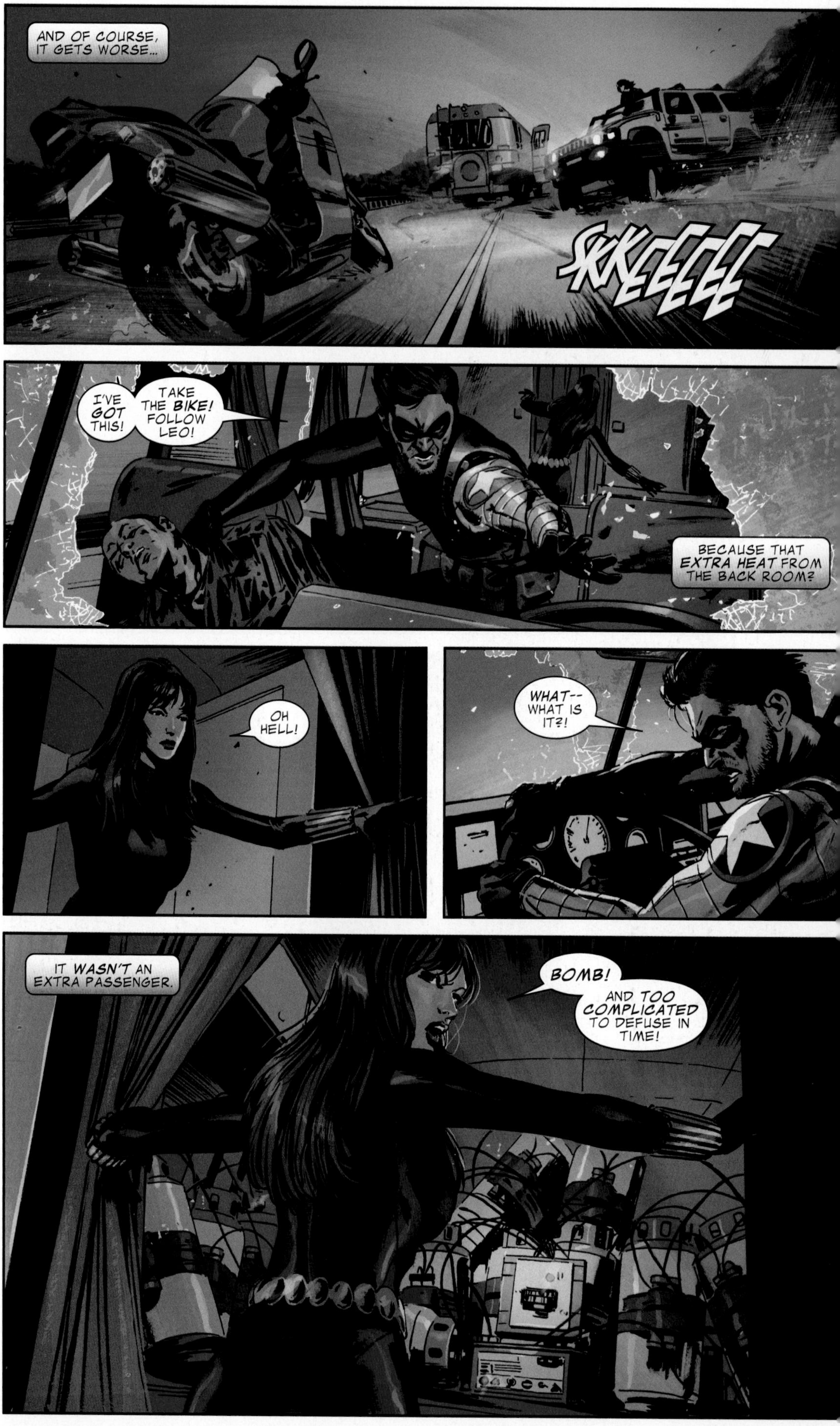
AND OF COURSE, IT GETS WORSE...
SKKEEEEE
I'VE GOT THIS!
TAKE THE BIKE! FOLLOW LEO!
BECAUSE THAT EXTRA HEAT FROM THE BACK ROOM?
OH HELL!
WHAT-- WHAT IS IT?!
IT WASN'T AN EXTRA PASSENGER.
BOMB!
AND TOO COMPLICATED TO DEFUSE IN TIME!

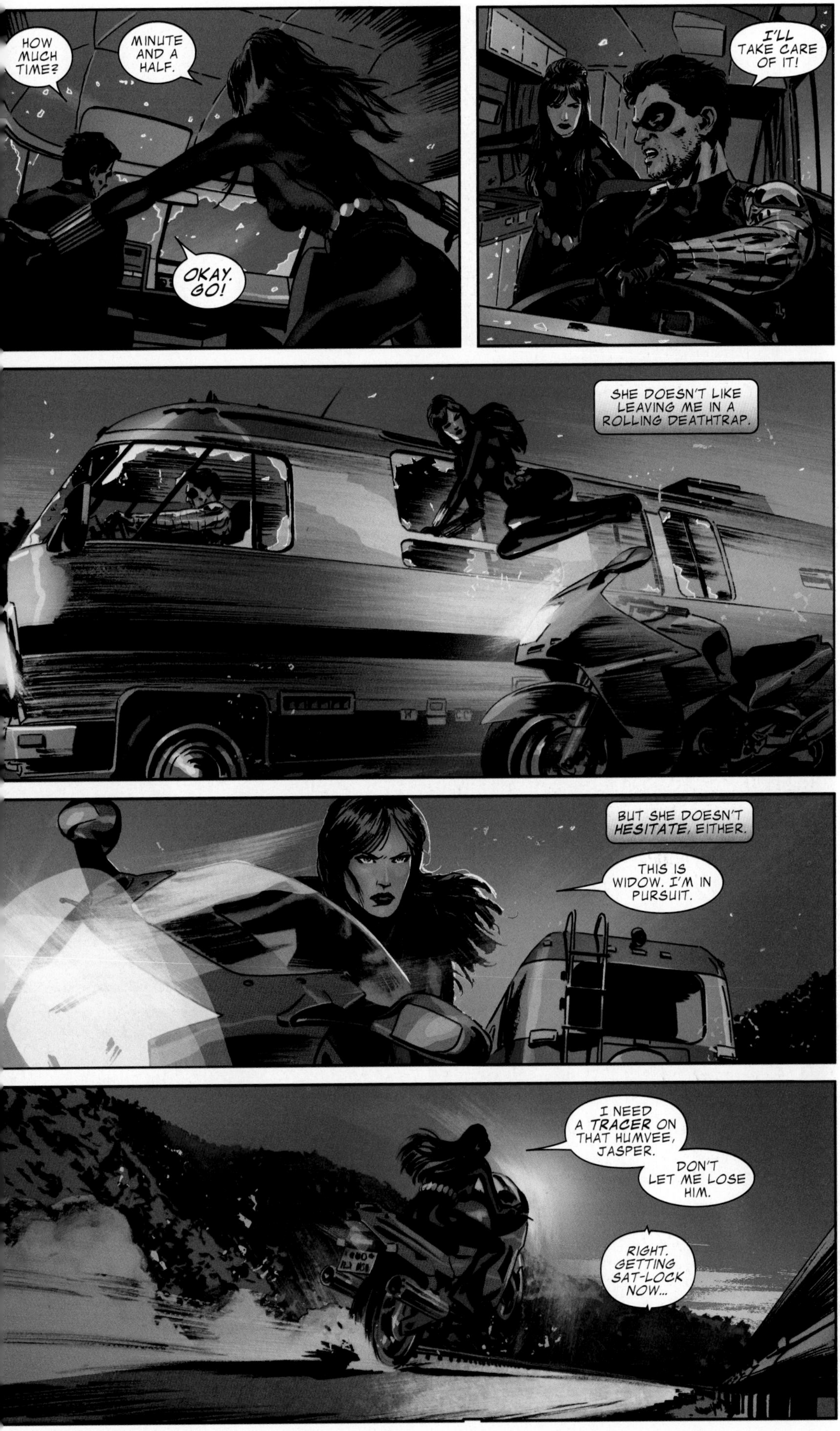
HOW MUCH TIME?
MINUTE AND A HALF.
OKAY. GO!
I'LL TAKE CARE OF IT!
SHE DOESN'T LIKE LEAVING ME IN A ROLLING DEATHTRAP.
BUT SHE DOESN'T HESITATE, EITHER.
THIS IS WIDOW. I'M IN PURSUIT.
I NEED A TRACER ON THAT HUMVEE, JASPER.
DON'T LET ME LOSE HIM.
RIGHT. GETTING SAT-LOCK NOW...

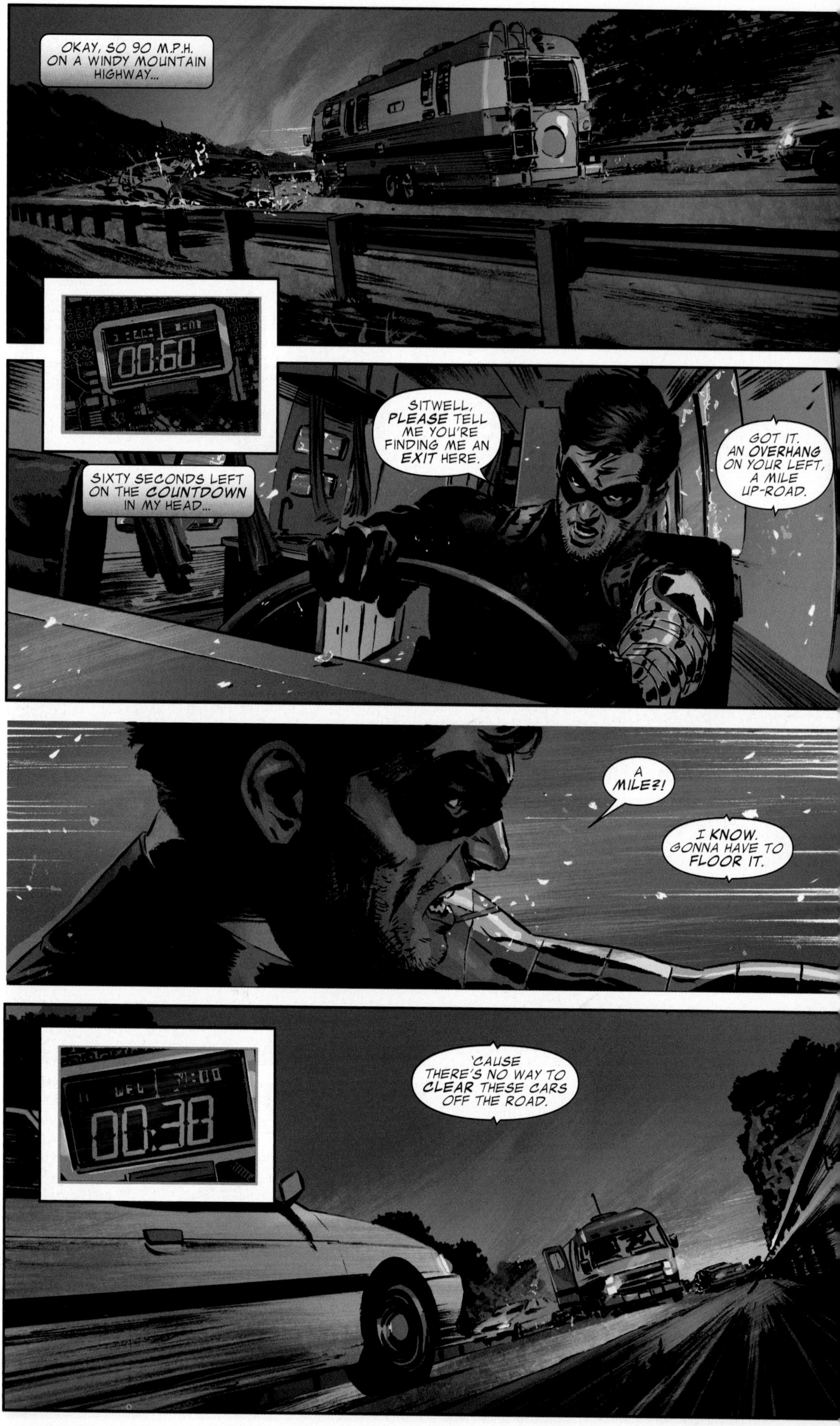
OKAY, SO 90 M.P.H. ON A WINDY MOUNTAIN HIGHWAY...
00:60
SIXTY SECONDS LEFT ON THE COUNTDOWN IN MY HEAD...
SITWELL, PLEASE TELL ME YOU'RE FINDING ME AN EXIT HERE.
GOT IT. AN OVERHANG ON YOUR LEFT, A MILE UP-ROAD.
A MILE?!
I KNOW. GONNA HAVE TO FLOOR IT.
00:38
'CAUSE THERE'S NO WAY TO CLEAR THESE CARS OFF THE ROAD.

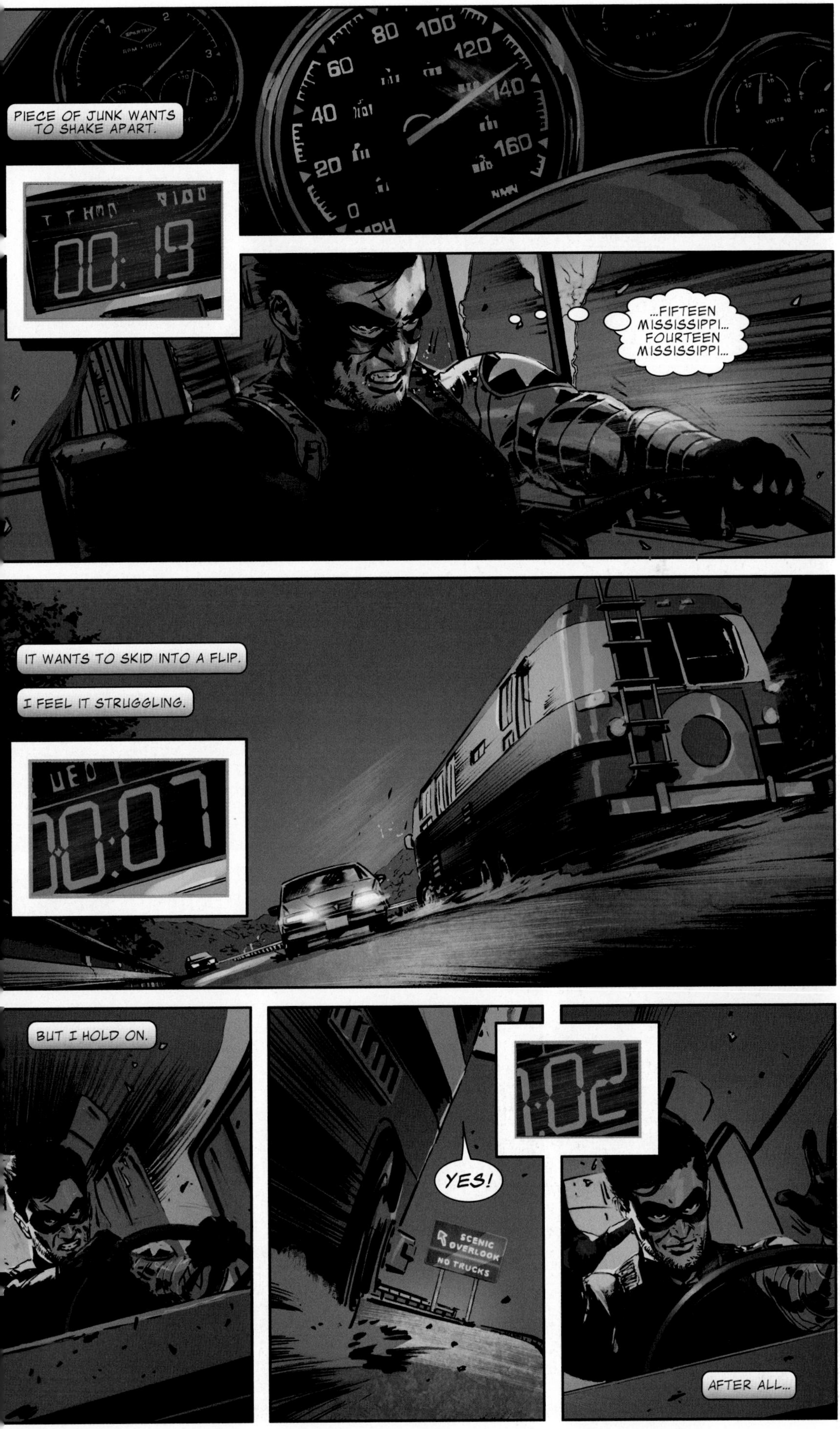

PIECE OF JUNK WANTS TO SHAKE APART.
00:13
...FIFTEEN MISSISSIPPI... FOURTEEN MISSISSIPPI...
IT WANTS TO SKID INTO A FLIP.
I FEEL IT STRUGGLING.
00:07
BUT I HOLD ON.
YES!
SCENIC OVERLOOK
NO TRUCKS
AFTER ALL...

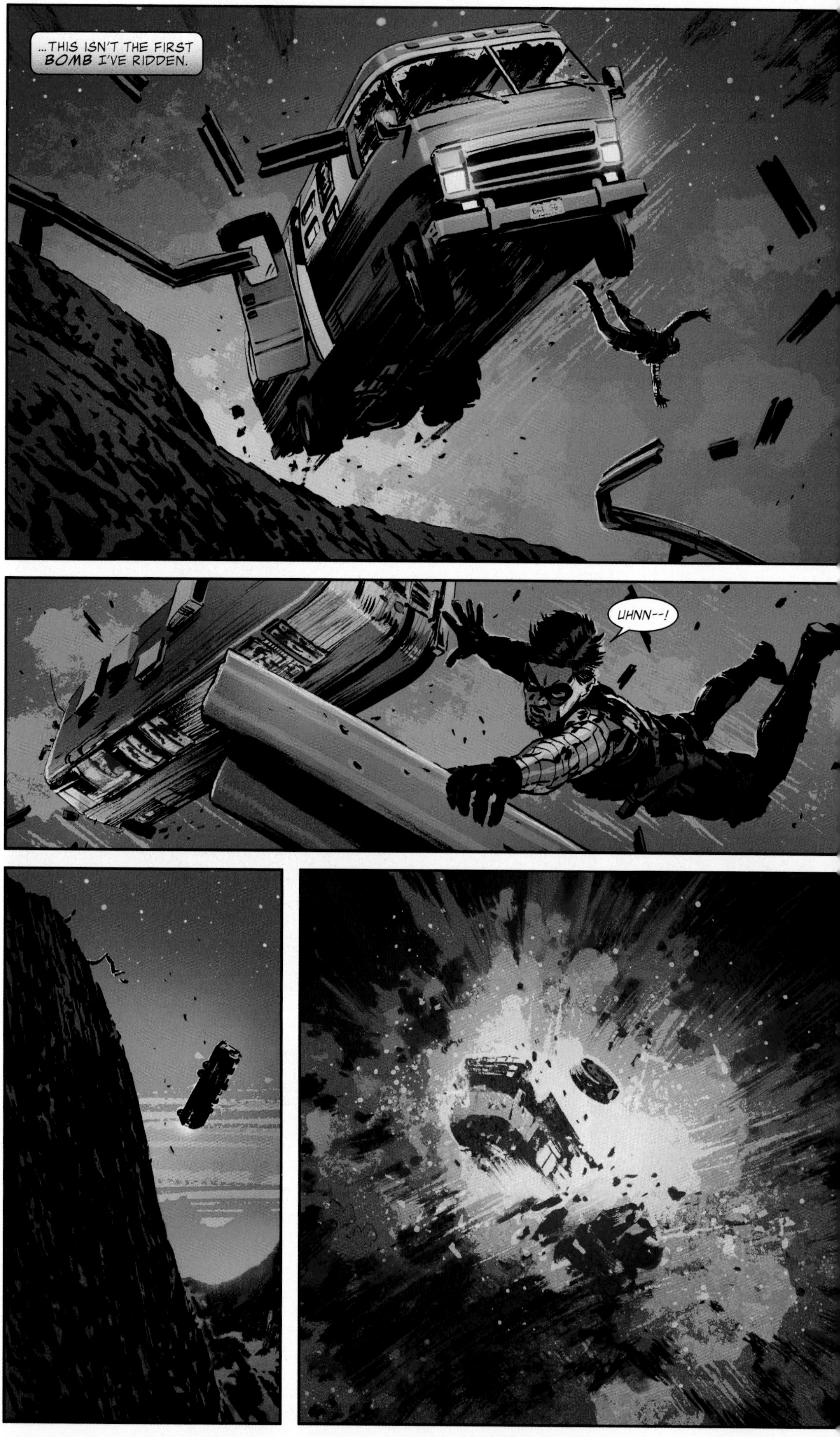
...THIS ISN'T THE FIRST BOMB I'VE RIDDEN.
UHNN--!

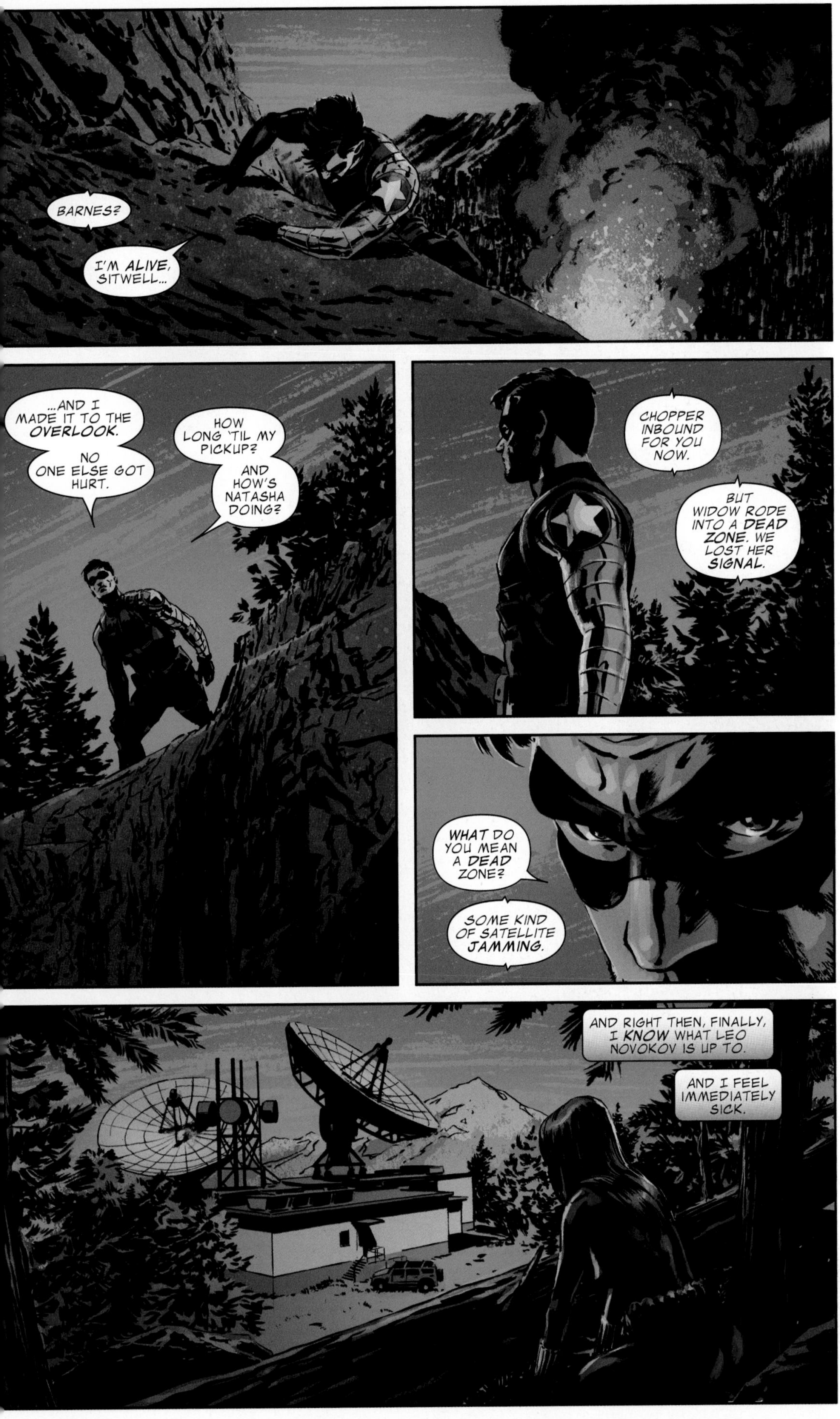
BARNES?
I'M ALIVE, SITWELL...
...AND I MADE IT TO THE OVERLOOK.
NO ONE ELSE GOT HURT.
HOW LONG 'TIL MY PICKUP?
AND HOW'S NATASHA DOING?
CHOPPER INBOUND FOR YOU NOW.
BUT WIDOW RODE INTO A DEAD ZONE. WE LOST HER SIGNAL.
WHAT DO YOU MEAN A DEAD ZONE?
SOME KIND OF SATELLITE JAMMING.
AND RIGHT THEN, FINALLY, I KNOW WHAT LEO NOVOKOV IS UP TO.
AND I FEEL IMMEDIATELY SICK.

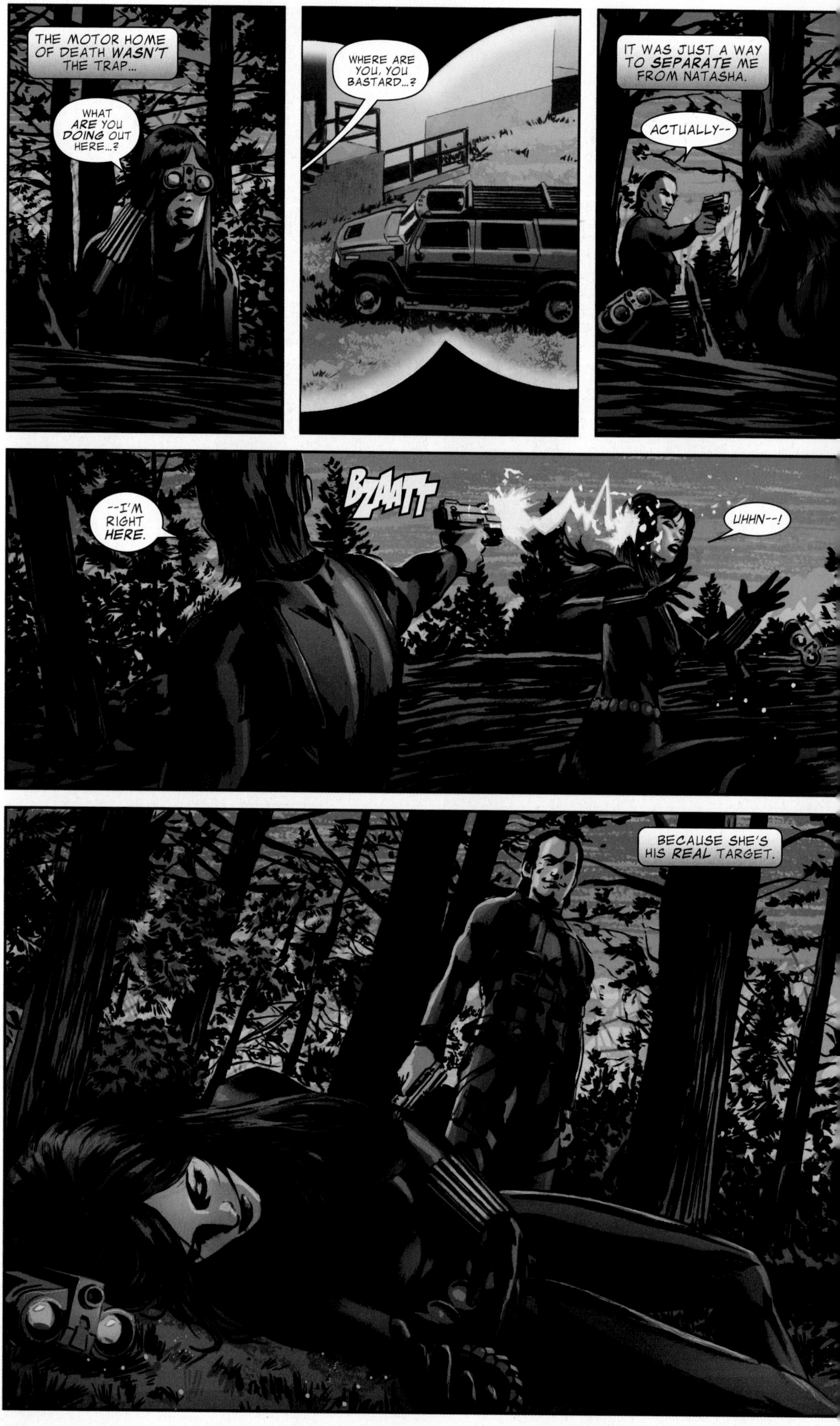
THE MOTOR HOME OF DEATH WASN'T THE TRAP...
WHAT ARE YOU DOING OUT HERE...?
WHERE ARE YOU, YOU BASTARD...?
IT WAS JUST A WAY TO SEPARATE ME FROM NATASHA.
ACTUALLY--
--I'M RIGHT HERE.
BZAATT
UHHN--!
BECAUSE SHE'S HIS REAL TARGET.

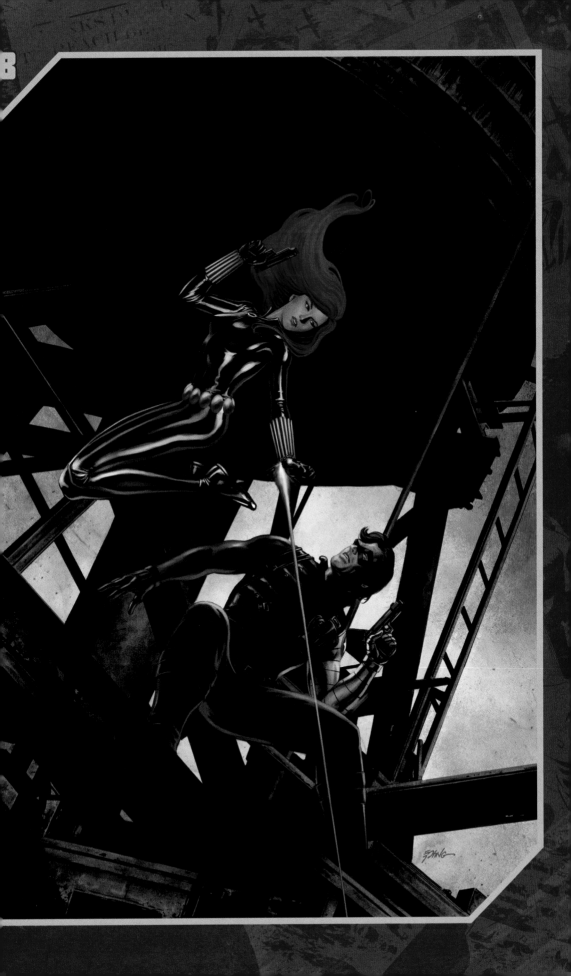

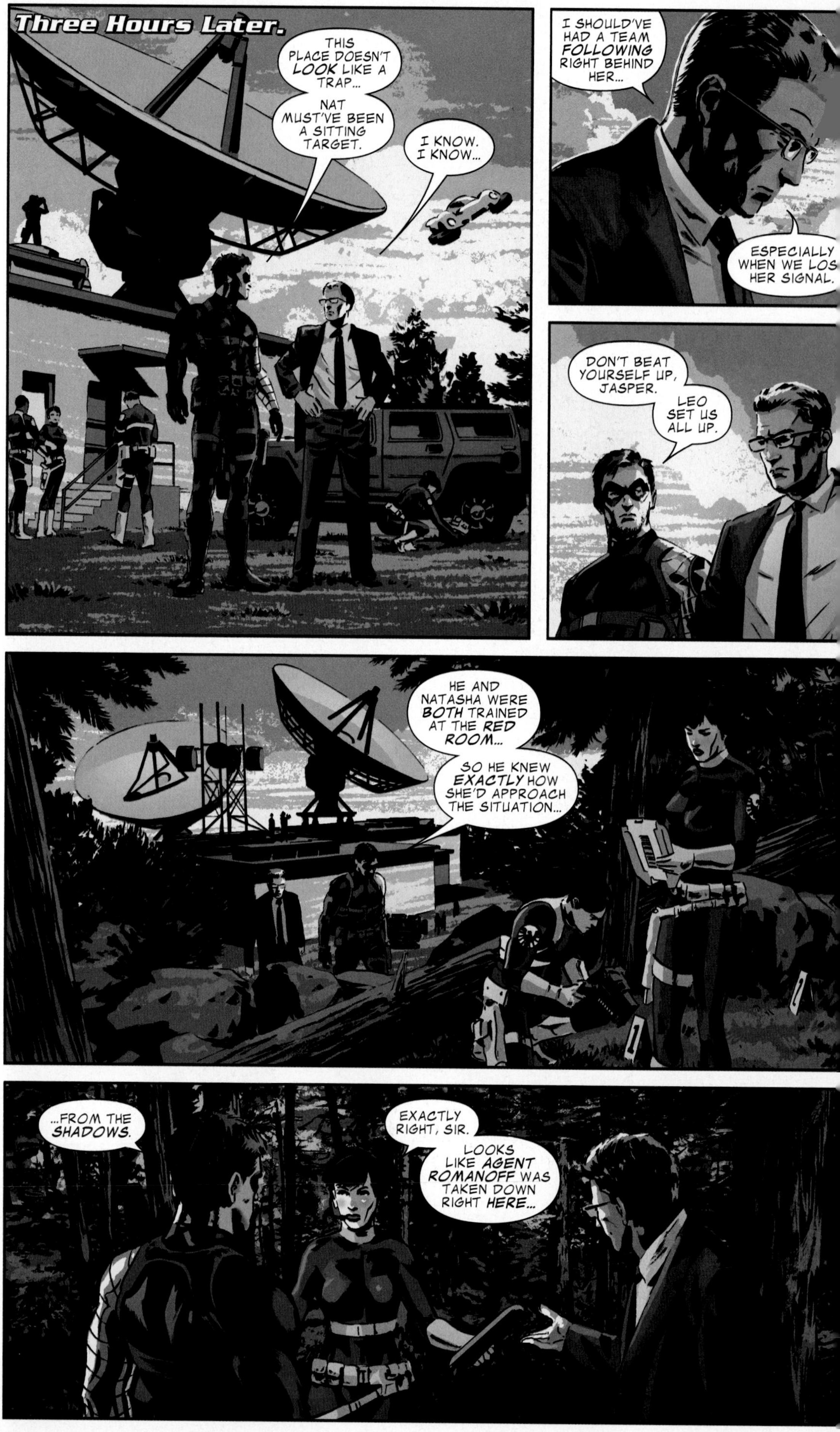
Three Hours Later.
THIS PLACE DOESN'T LOOK LIKE A TRAP...
NAT MUST'VE BEEN A SITTING TARGET.
I KNOW. I KNOW...
I SHOULD'VE HAD A TEAM FOLLOWING RIGHT BEHIND HER...
ESPECIALLY WHEN WE LOS HER SIGNAL.
DON'T BEAT YOURSELF UP, JASPER.
LEO SET US ALL UP.
HE AND NATASHA WERE BOTH TRAINED AT THE RED ROOM...
SO HE KNEW EXACTLY HOW SHE'D APPROACH THE SITUATION...
...FROM THE SHADOWS.
EXACTLY RIGHT, SIR.
LOOKS LIKE AGENT ROMANOFF WAS TAKEN DOWN RIGHT HERE...

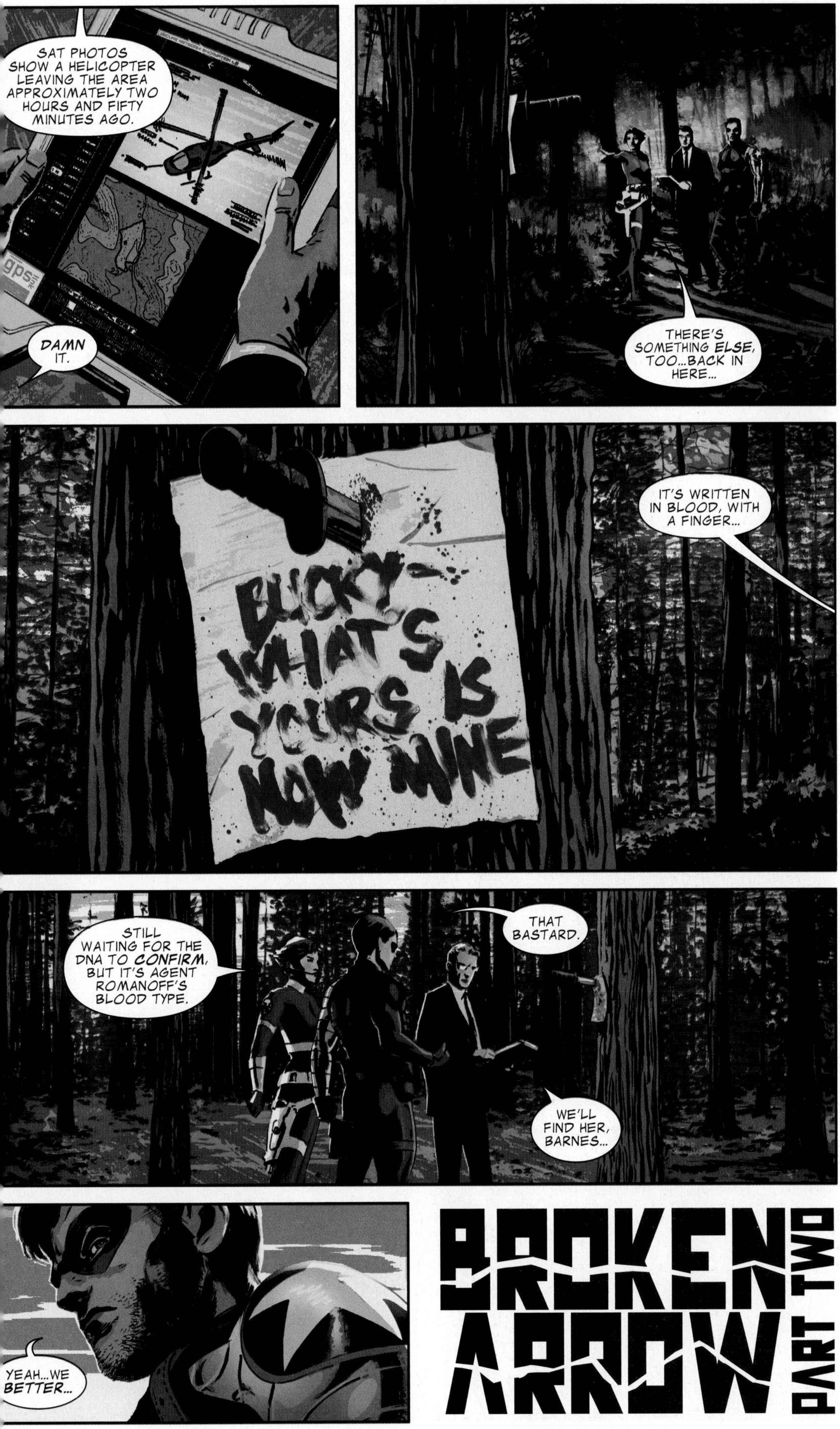
SAT PHOTOS SHOW A HELICOPTER LEAVING THE AREA APPROXIMATELY TWO HOURS AND FIFTY MINUTES AGO.
DAMN IT.
THERE'S SOMETHING ELSE, TOO...BACK IN HERE...
BUCKY- WHATS YOURS IS NOW MINE
IT'S WRITTEN IN BLOOD, WITH A FINGER...
STILL WAITING FOR THE DNA TO CONFIRM, BUT IT'S AGENT ROMANOFF'S BLOOD TYPE.
THAT BASTARD.
WE'LL FIND HER, BARNES...
YEAH...WE BETTER...
BROKEN ARROW
PART TWO

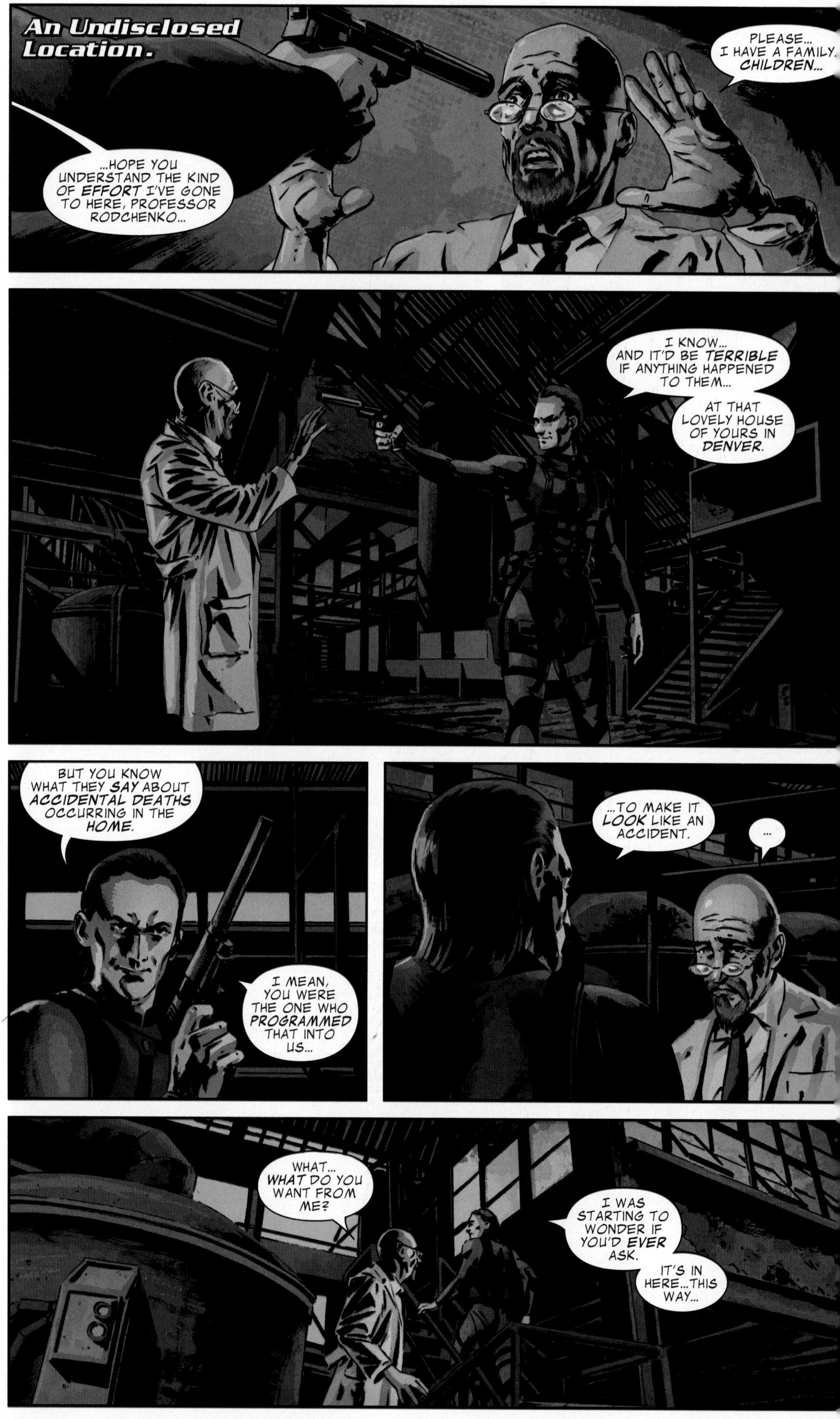
An Undisclosed Location.
...HOPE YOU UNDERSTAND THE KIND OF EFFORT I'VE GONE TO HERE, PROFESSOR RODCHENKO...
PLEASE... I HAVE A FAMILY. CHILDREN...
I KNOW... AND IT'D BE TERRIBLE IF ANYTHING HAPPENED TO THEM...
AT THAT LOVELY HOUSE OF YOURS IN DENVER.
BUT YOU KNOW WHAT THEY SAY ABOUT ACCIDENTAL DEATHS OCCURRING IN THE HOME.
I MEAN, YOU WERE THE ONE WHO PROGRAMMED THAT INTO US...
...TO MAKE IT LOOK LIKE AN ACCIDENT.
...
WHAT... WHAT DO YOU WANT FROM ME?
I WAS STARTING TO WONDER IF YOU'D EVER ASK.
IT'S IN HERE...THIS WAY...

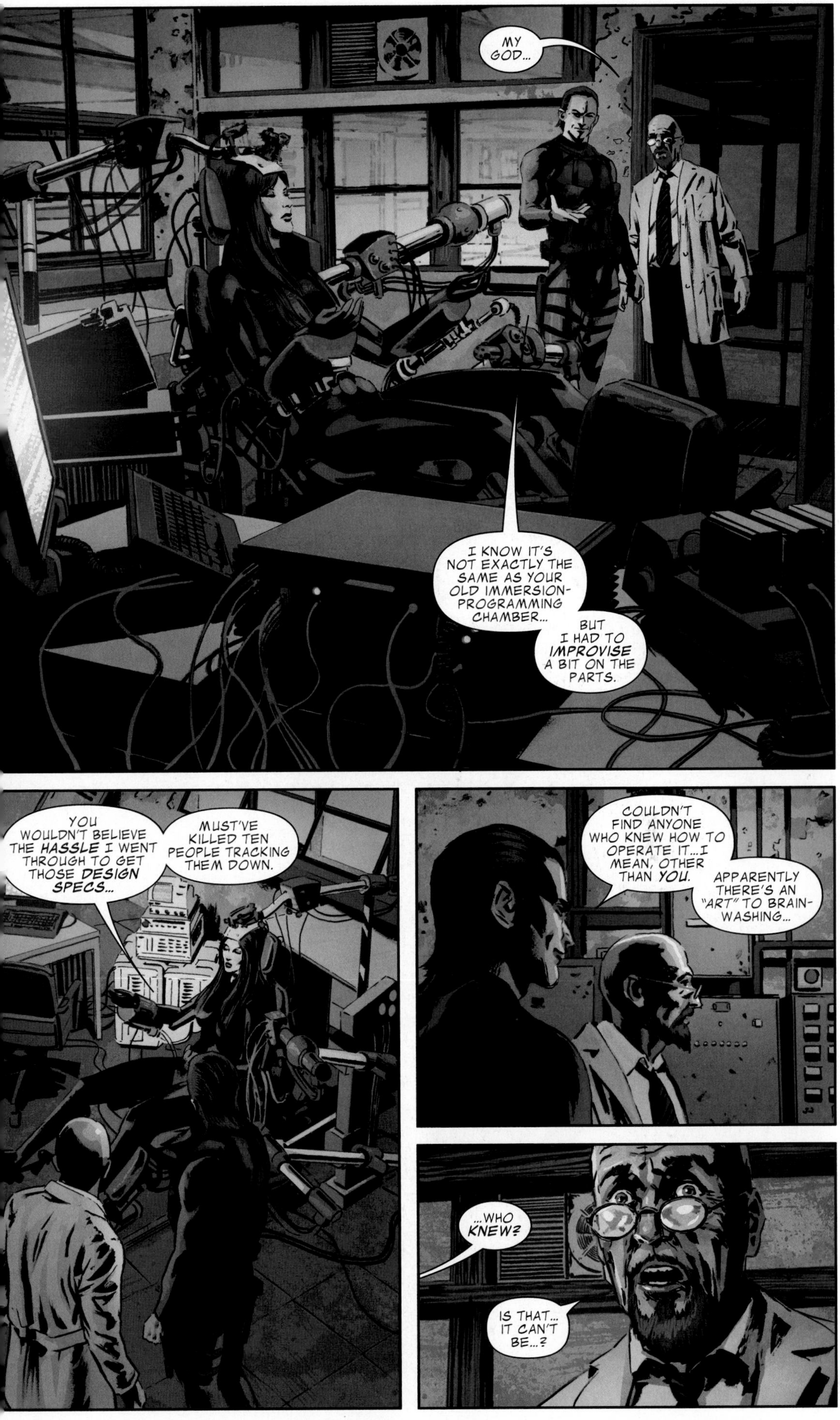
MY GOD...
I KNOW IT'S NOT EXACTLY THE SAME AS YOUR OLD IMMERSION-PROGRAMMING CHAMBER...
BUT I HAD TO IMPROVISE A BIT ON THE PARTS.
YOU WOULDN'T BELIEVE THE HASSLE I WENT THROUGH TO GET THOSE DESIGN SPECS...
MUST'VE KILLED TEN PEOPLE TRACKING THEM DOWN.
COULDN'T FIND ANYONE WHO KNEW HOW TO OPERATE IT...I MEAN, OTHER THAN YOU.
APPARENTLY THERE'S AN "ART" TO BRAIN-WASHING...
...WHO KNEW?
IS THAT... IT CAN'T BE...?

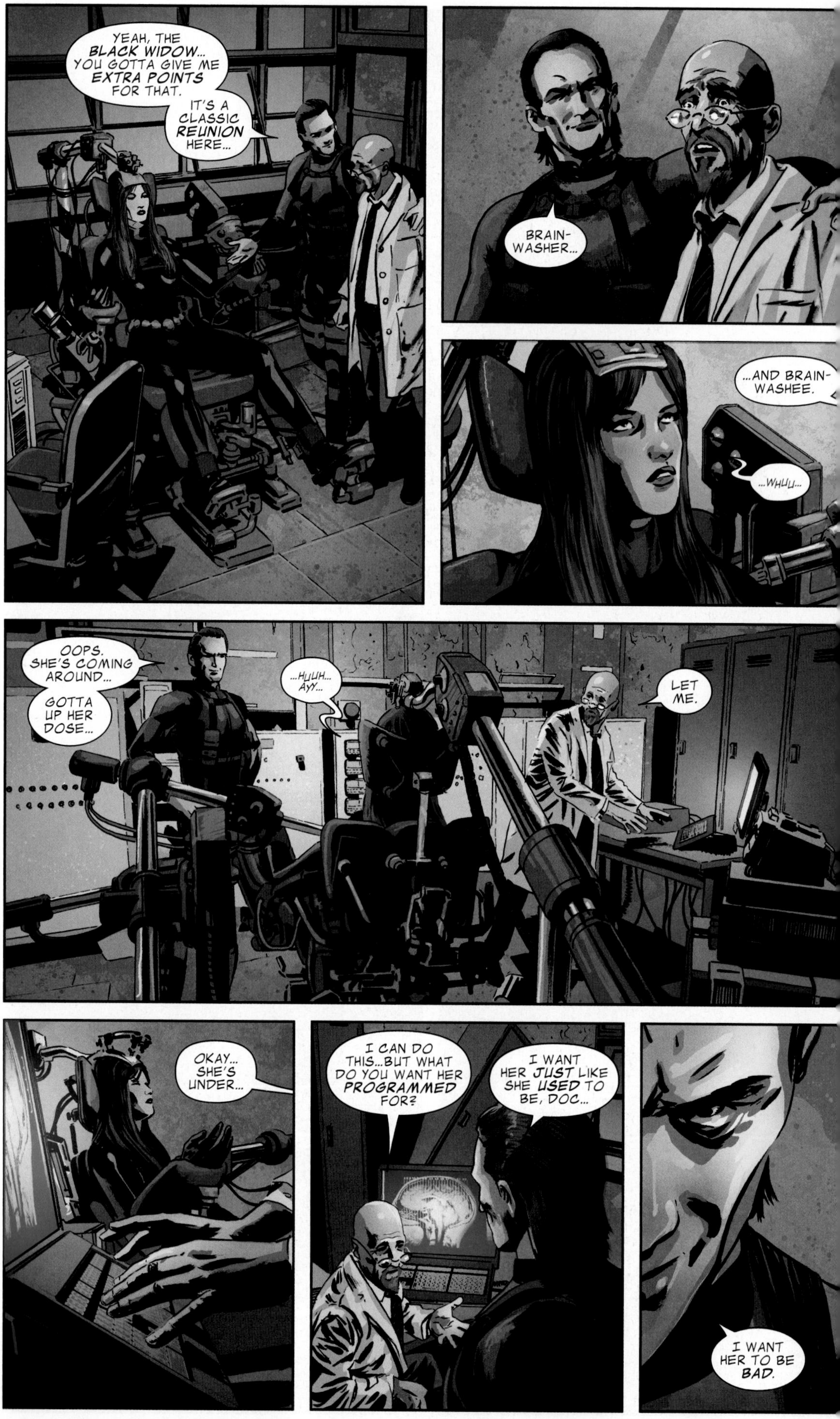

YEAH, THE BLACK WIDOW... YOU GOTTA GIVE ME EXTRA POINTS FOR THAT.
IT'S A CLASSIC REUNION HERE...
BRAIN-WASHER...
...AND BRAIN-WASHEE.
...WHUU...
OOPS. SHE'S COMING AROUND...
GOTTA UP HER DOSE...
...HUUH... AYY...
LET ME.
OKAY... SHE'S UNDER...
I CAN DO THIS...BUT WHAT DO YOU WANT HER PROGRAMMED FOR?
I WANT HER JUST LIKE SHE USED TO BE, DOC...
I WANT HER TO BE BAD.

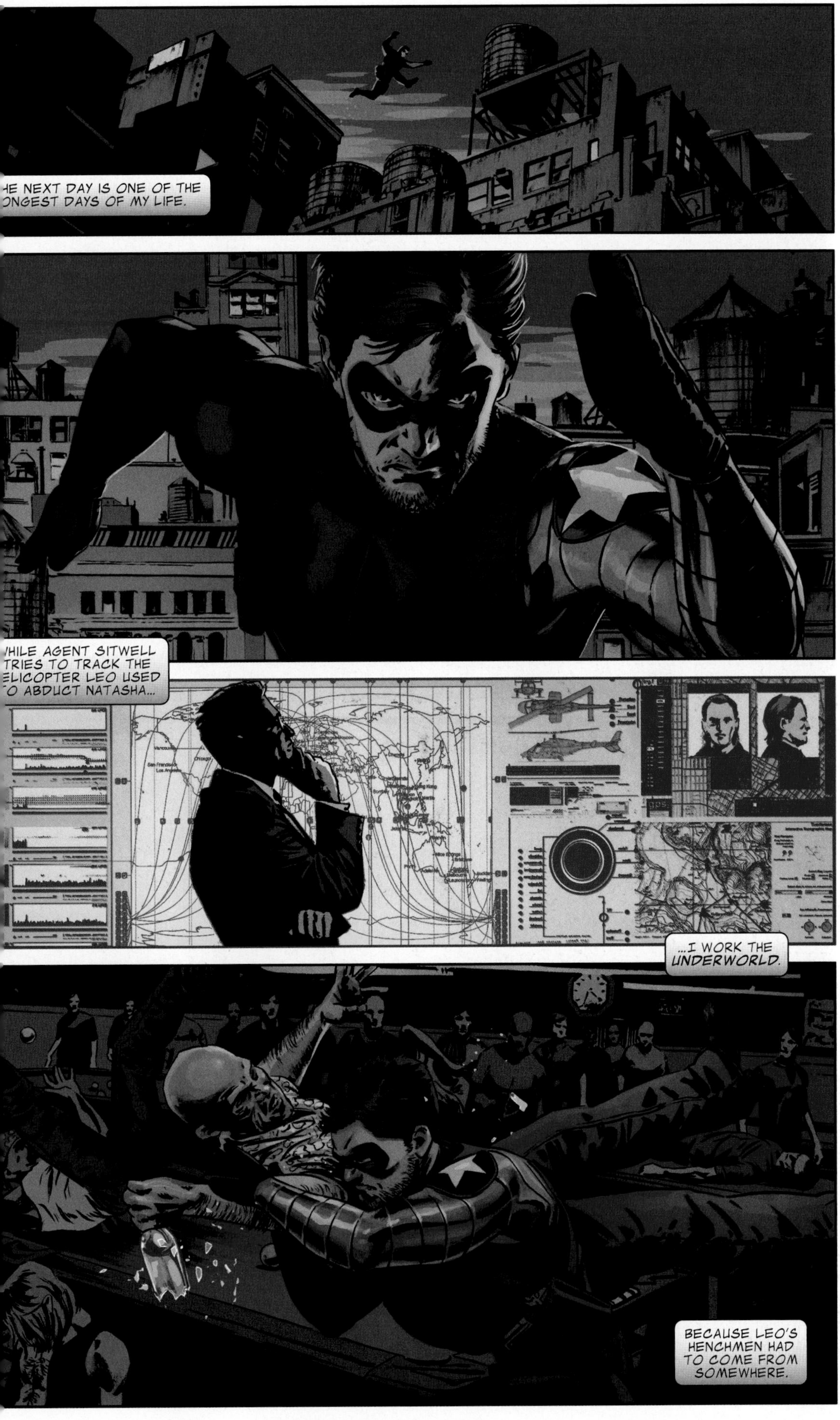
HE NEXT DAY IS ONE OF THE ONGEST DAYS OF MY LIFE.
WHILE AGENT SITWELL TRIES TO TRACK THE ELICOPTER LEO USED O ABDUCT NATASHA...
...I WORK THE UNDERWORLD.
BECAUSE LEO'S HENCHMEN HAD TO COME FROM SOMEWHERE.

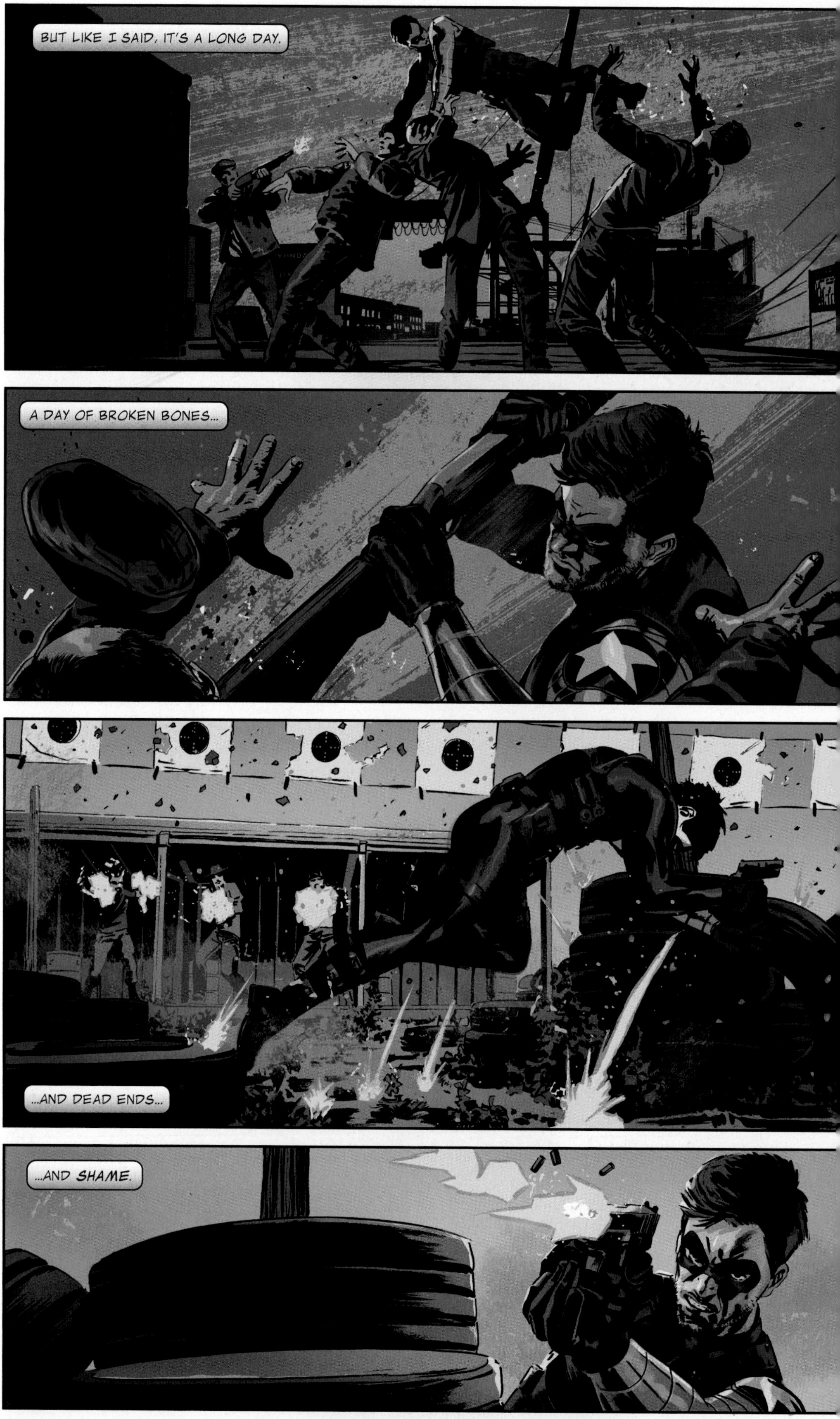
BUT LIKE I SAID, IT'S A LONG DAY.
A DAY OF BROKEN BONES...
...AND DEAD ENDS...
...AND SHAME.

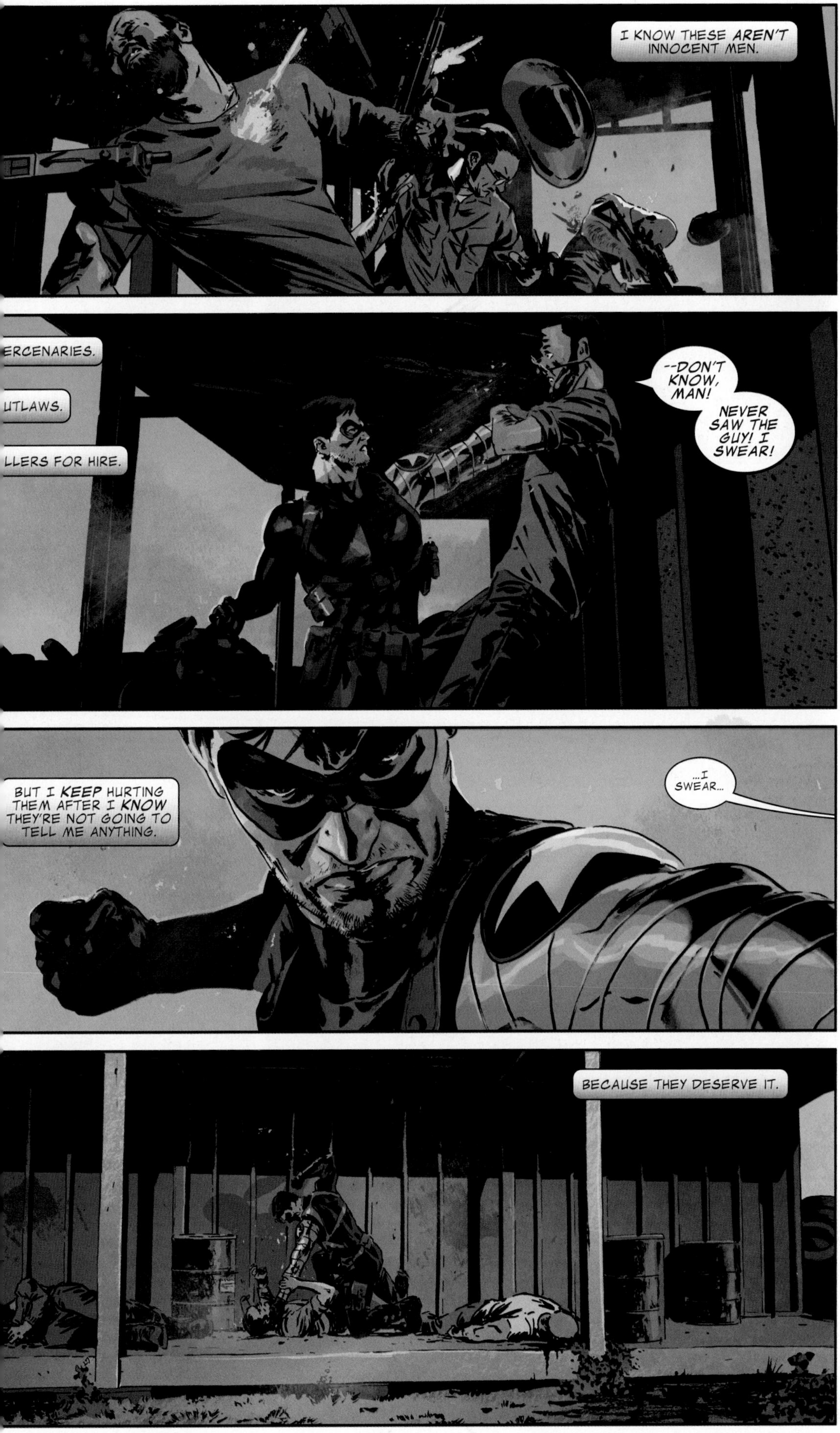
I KNOW THESE AREN'T INNOCENT MEN.
ERCENARIES.
UTLAWS.
LLERS FOR HIRE.
--DON'T KNOW, MAN!
NEVER SAW THE GUY! I SWEAR!
BUT I KEEP HURTING THEM AFTER I KNOW THEY'RE NOT GOING TO TELL ME ANYTHING.
...I SWEAR...
BECAUSE THEY DESERVE IT.

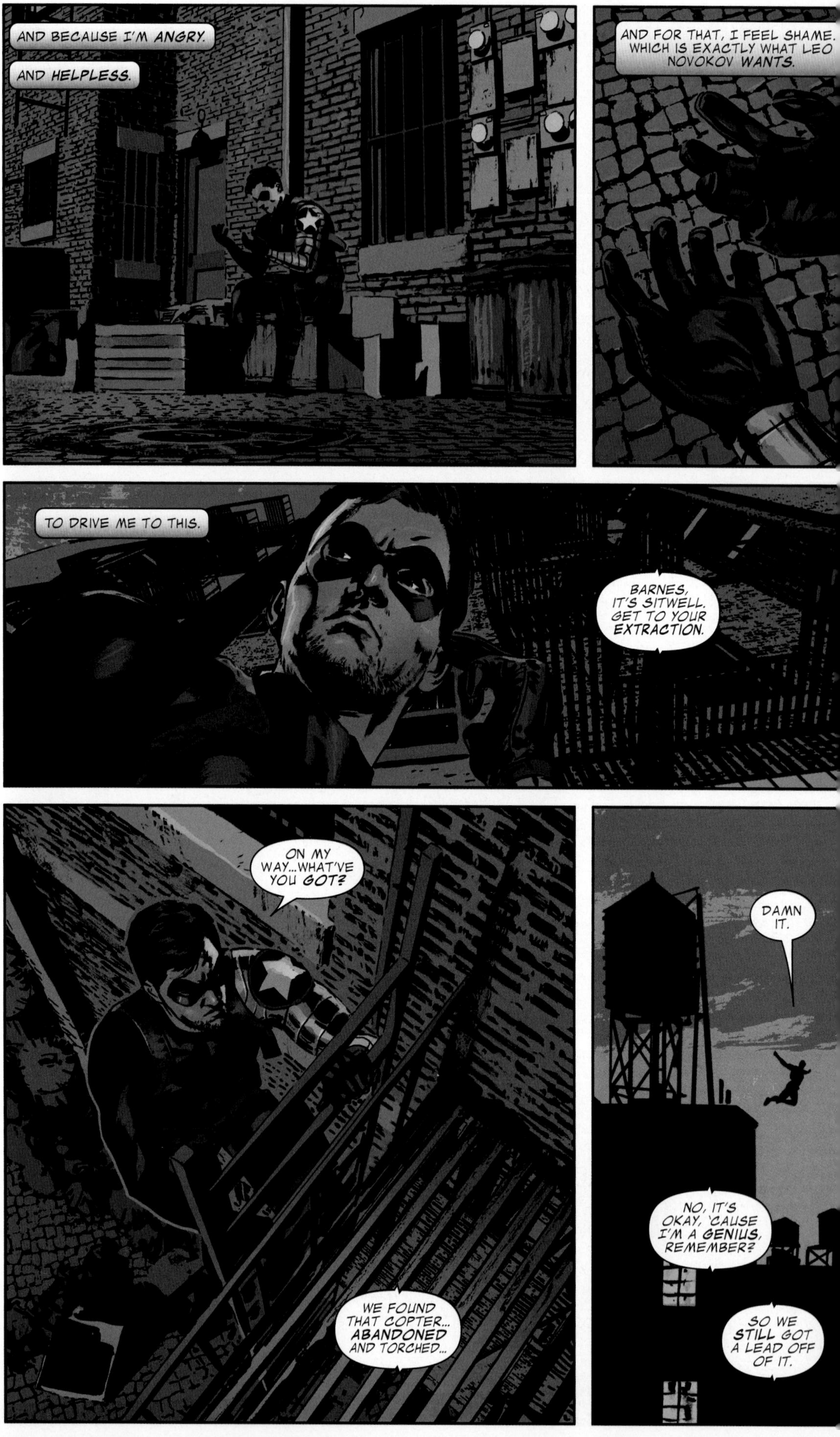
AND BECAUSE I'M ANGRY.
AND HELPLESS.
AND FOR THAT, I FEEL SHAME. WHICH IS EXACTLY WHAT LEO NOVOKOV WANTS.
TO DRIVE ME TO THIS.
BARNES, IT'S SITWELL. GET TO YOUR EXTRACTION.
ON MY WAY...WHAT'VE YOU GOT?
WE FOUND THAT COPTER... ABANDONED AND TORCHED...
DAMN IT.
NO, IT'S OKAY, 'CAUSE I'M A GENIUS, REMEMBER?
SO WE STILL GOT A LEAD OFF OF IT.

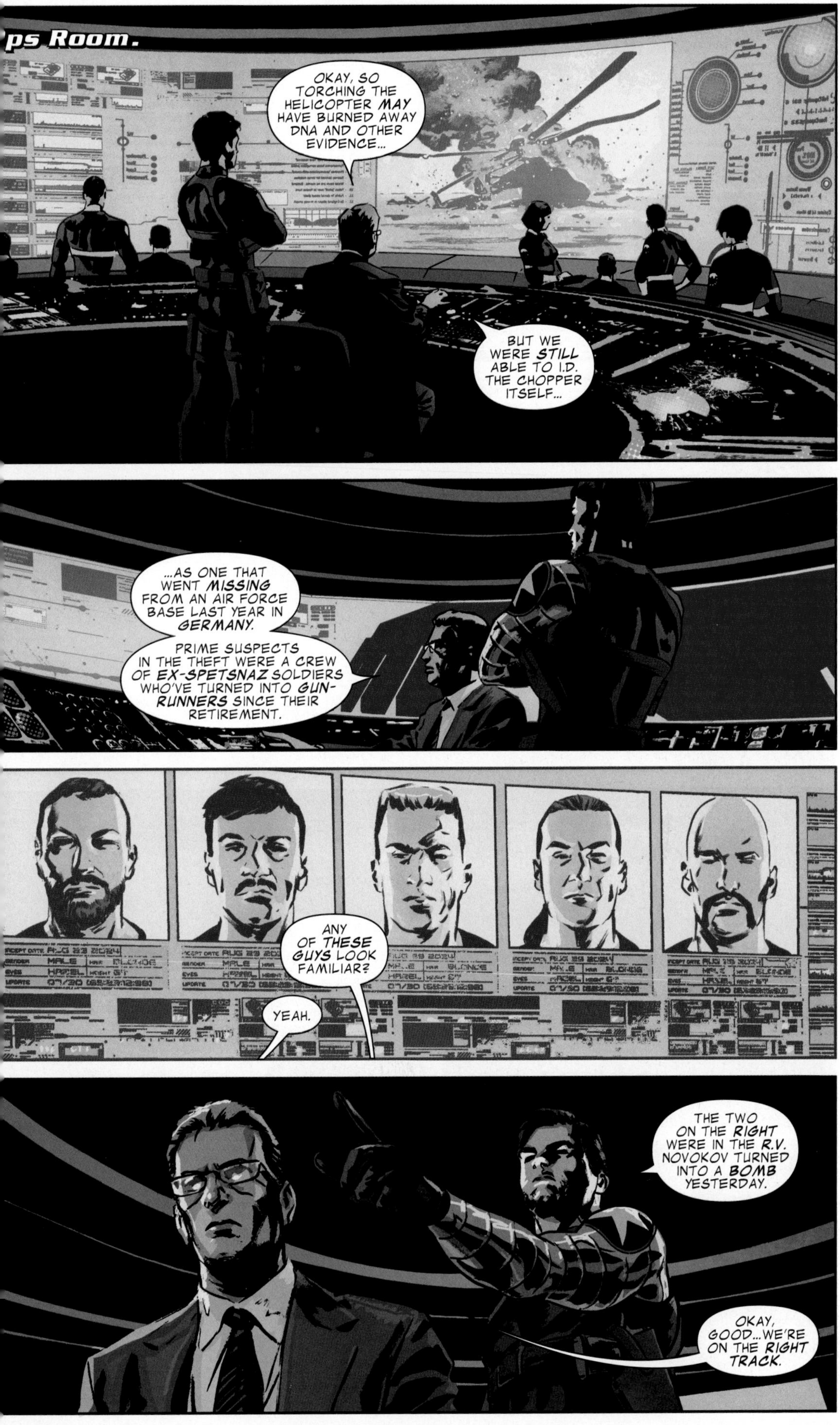
ps Room.
OKAY, SO TORCHING THE HELICOPTER MAY HAVE BURNED AWAY DNA AND OTHER EVIDENCE...
BUT WE WERE STILL ABLE TO I.D. THE CHOPPER ITSELF...
...AS ONE THAT WENT MISSING FROM AN AIR FORCE BASE LAST YEAR IN GERMANY.
PRIME SUSPECTS IN THE THEFT WERE A CREW OF EX-SPETSNAZ SOLDIERS WHO'VE TURNED INTO GUN-RUNNERS SINCE THEIR RETIREMENT.
ANY OF THESE GUYS LOOK FAMILIAR?
YEAH.
THE TWO ON THE RIGHT WERE IN THE R.V. NOVOKOV TURNED INTO A BOMB YESTERDAY.
OKAY, GOOD...WE'RE ON THE RIGHT TRACK.

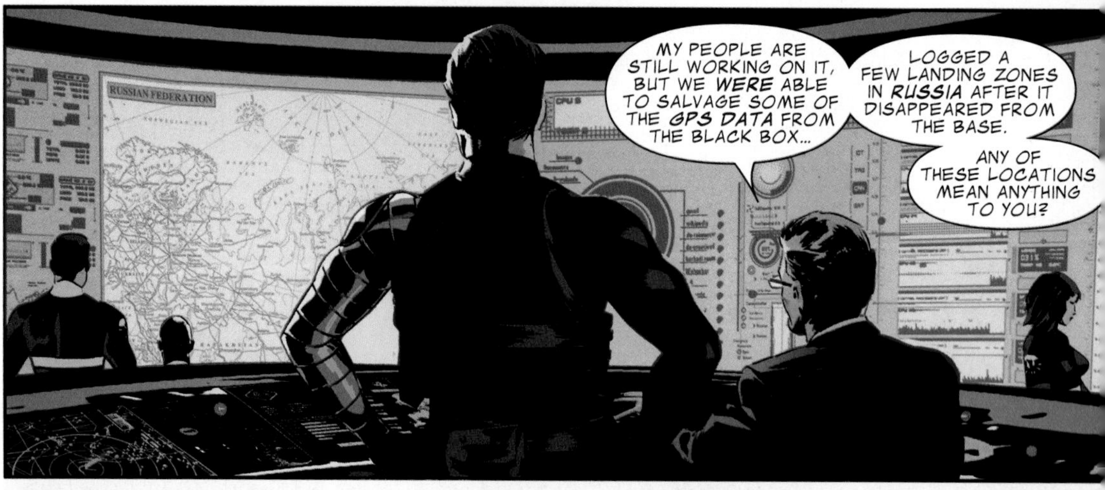
RUSSIAN FEDERATION
MY PEOPLE ARE STILL WORKING ON IT, BUT WE WERE ABLE TO SALVAGE SOME OF THE GPS DATA FROM THE BLACK BOX...
LOGGED A FEW LANDING ZONES IN RUSSIA AFTER IT DISAPPEARED FROM THE BASE.
ANY OF THESE LOCATIONS MEAN ANYTHING TO YOU?

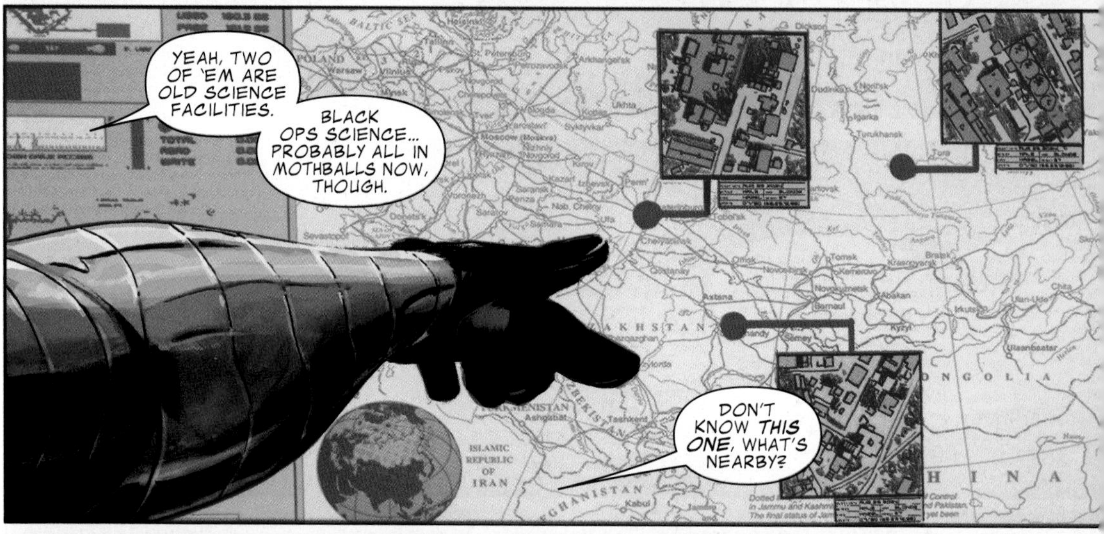
YEAH, TWO OF 'EM ARE OLD SCIENCE FACILITIES.
BLACK OPS SCIENCE... PROBABLY ALL IN MOTHBALLS NOW, THOUGH.
DON'T KNOW THIS ONE, WHAT'S NEARBY?

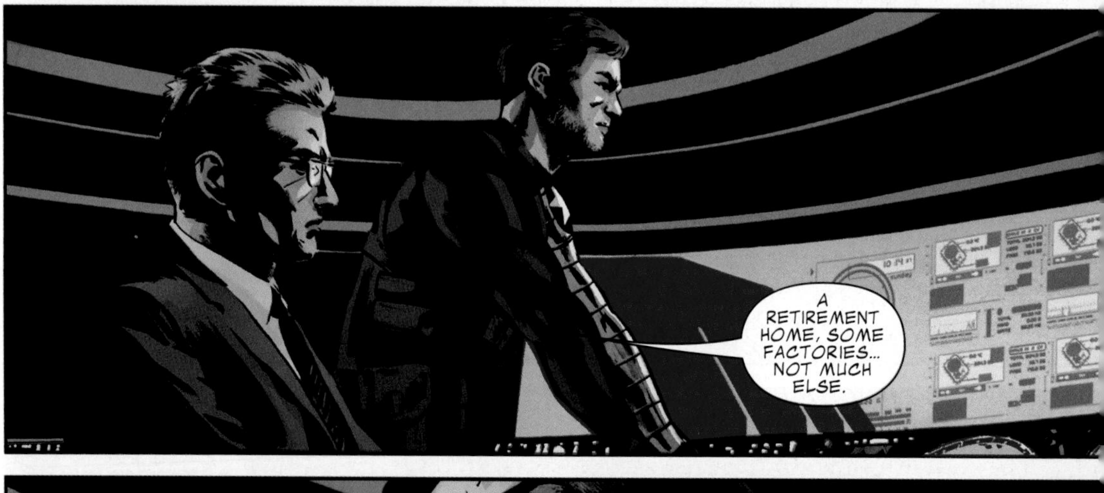
A RETIREMENT HOME, SOME FACTORIES... NOT MUCH ELSE.

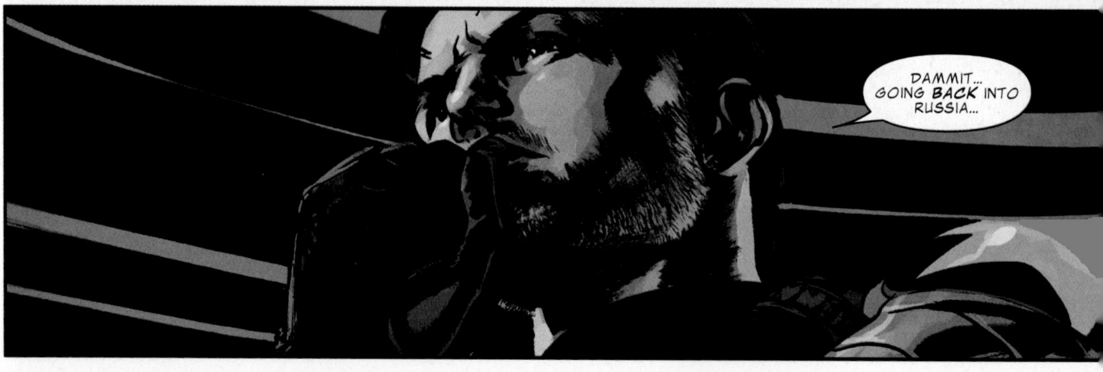
DAMMIT... GOING BACK INTO RUSSIA...

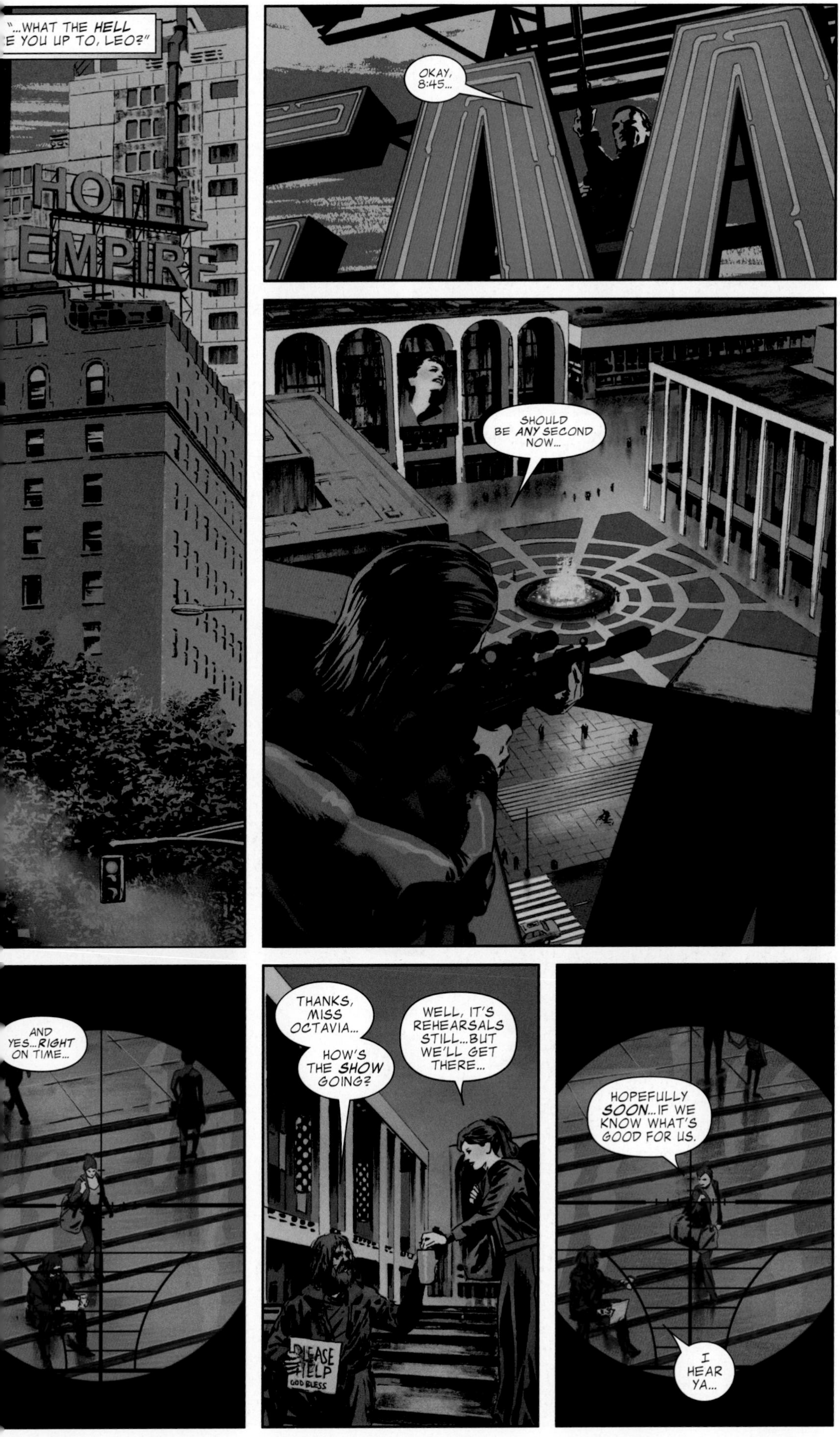
"...WHAT THE HELL
E YOU UP TO, LEO?"
HOTEL EMPIRE
OKAY, 8:45...
SHOULD BE ANY SECOND NOW...
AND YES...RIGHT ON TIME...
THANKS, MISS OCTAVIA...
HOW'S THE SHOW GOING?
WELL, IT'S REHEARSALS STILL...BUT WE'LL GET THERE...
PLEASE HELP
GOD BLESS
HOPEFULLY SOON...IF WE KNOW WHAT'S GOOD FOR US.
I HEAR YA...

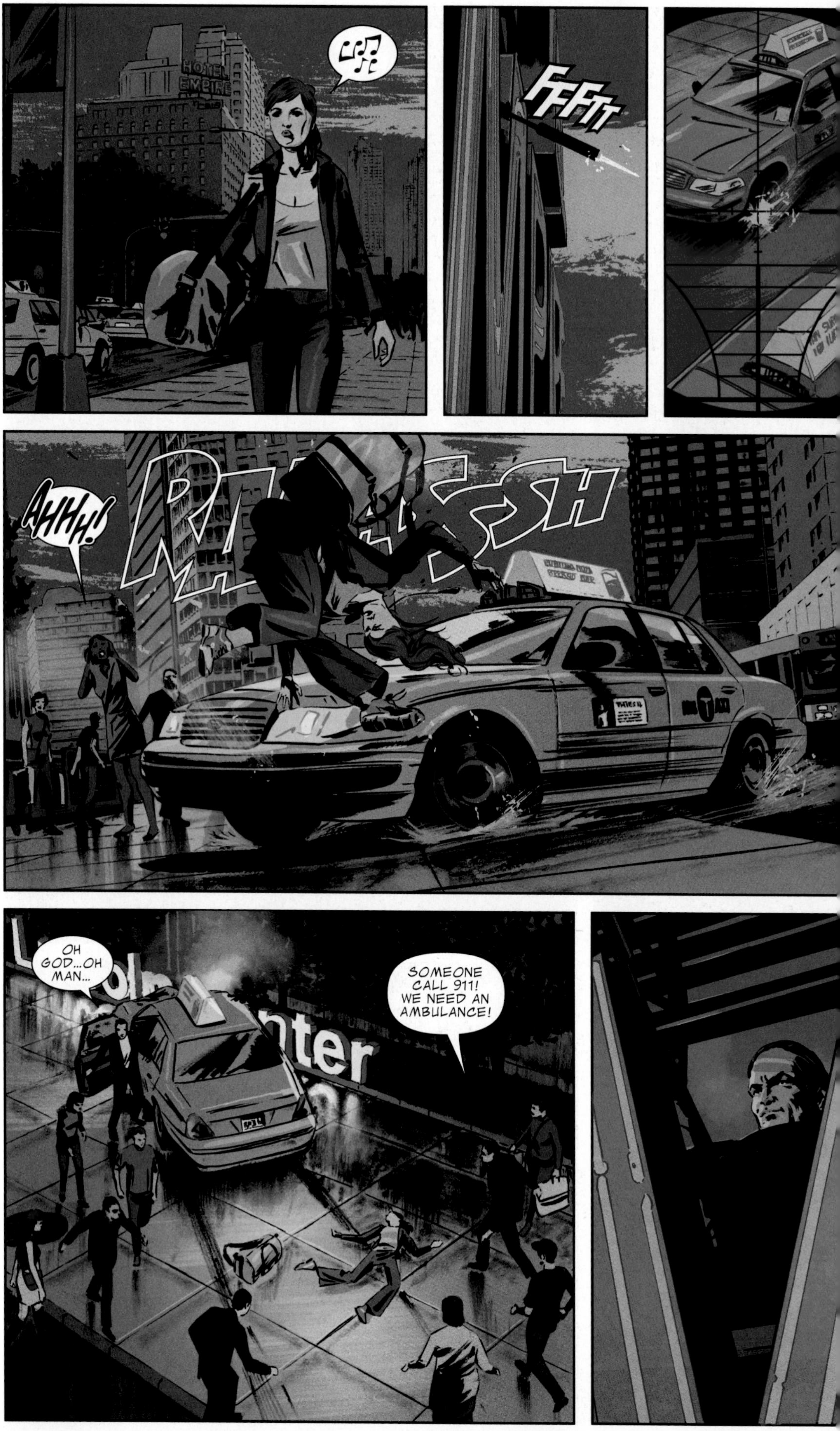
HOTEL EMPIRE
FFFTT
AHHH!
OH GOD...OH MAN...
SOMEONE CALL 911! WE NEED AN AMBULANCE!

SO, HOW'RE YOU HOLDIN' UP?

ME? FINE.

PLEASE, BARNES...BE REAL.

YOU'RE A WRECK.

WHAT'RE WE, FRIENDS ALL OF A SUDDEN?

YEAH. WE ARE.

OH. OKAY THEN... I GUESS.

Y'KNOW, I'VE TECHNICALLY KNOWN NATASHA LONGER THAN YOU HAVE...

WORKED TOGETHER ON AND OFF... NEARLY TEN YEARS...

WHAT'RE YOU GETTING AT HERE, JASPER?

NO. NOT THAT...I'M NOT CRAZY ENOUGH TO BE IN LOVE WITH HER.

HEY.

NO OFFENSE.

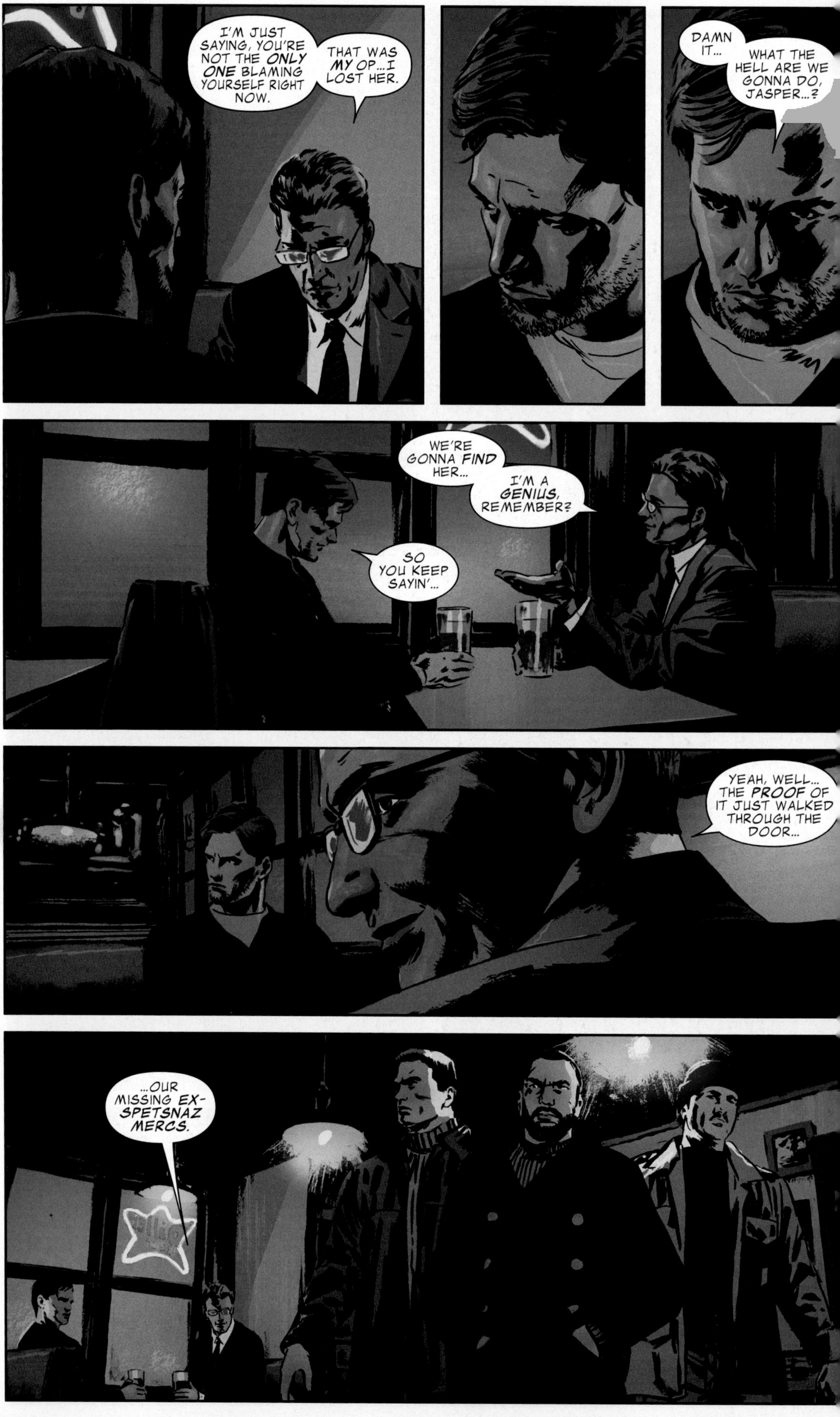
I'M JUST SAYING, YOU'RE NOT THE ONLY ONE BLAMING YOURSELF RIGHT NOW.
THAT WAS MY OP...I LOST HER.
DAMN IT...
WHAT THE HELL ARE WE GONNA DO, JASPER...?
WE'RE GONNA FIND HER...
I'M A GENIUS, REMEMBER?
SO YOU KEEP SAYIN'...
YEAH, WELL... THE PROOF OF IT JUST WALKED THROUGH THE DOOR...
...OUR MISSING EX-SPETSNAZ MERCS.

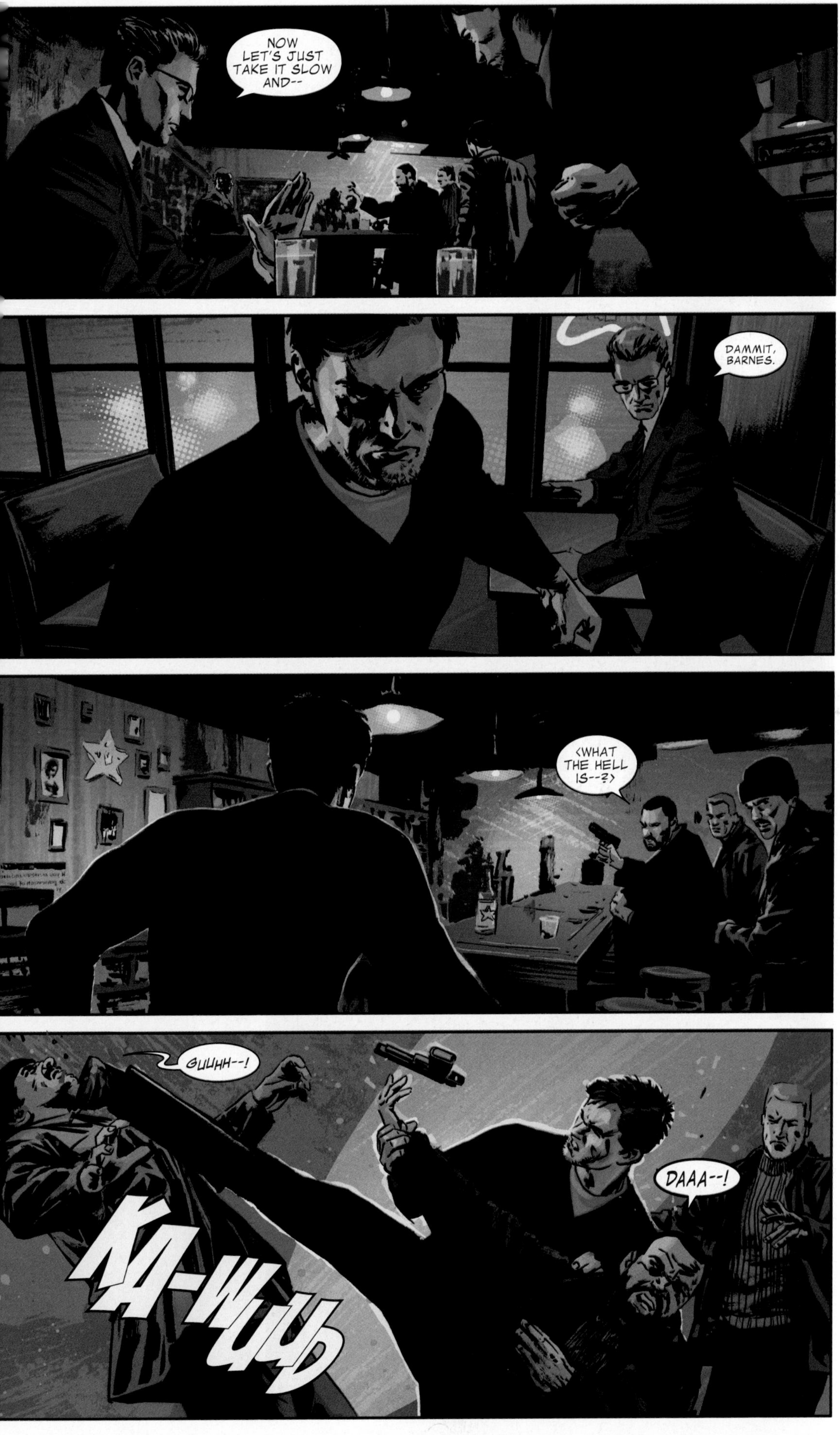
NOW LET'S JUST TAKE IT SLOW AND--
DAMMIT, BARNES.
<WHAT THE HELL IS--?>
GUUHH--!
DAAA--!
KA-WUUD

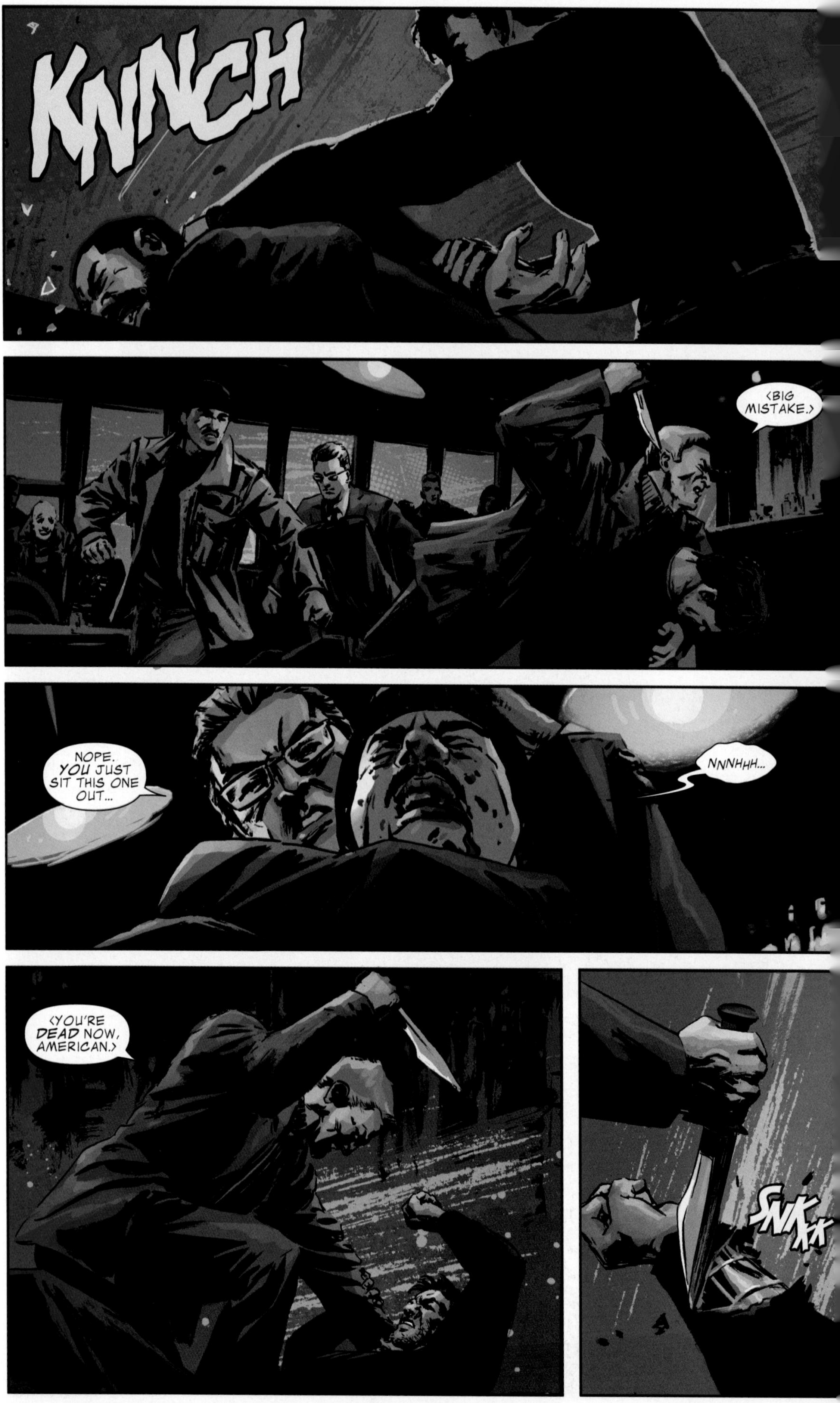
KNNCH
<BIG MISTAKE.>
NOPE. YOU JUST SIT THIS ONE OUT...
NNNHHH...
<YOU'RE DEAD NOW, AMERICAN.>
SNKKK

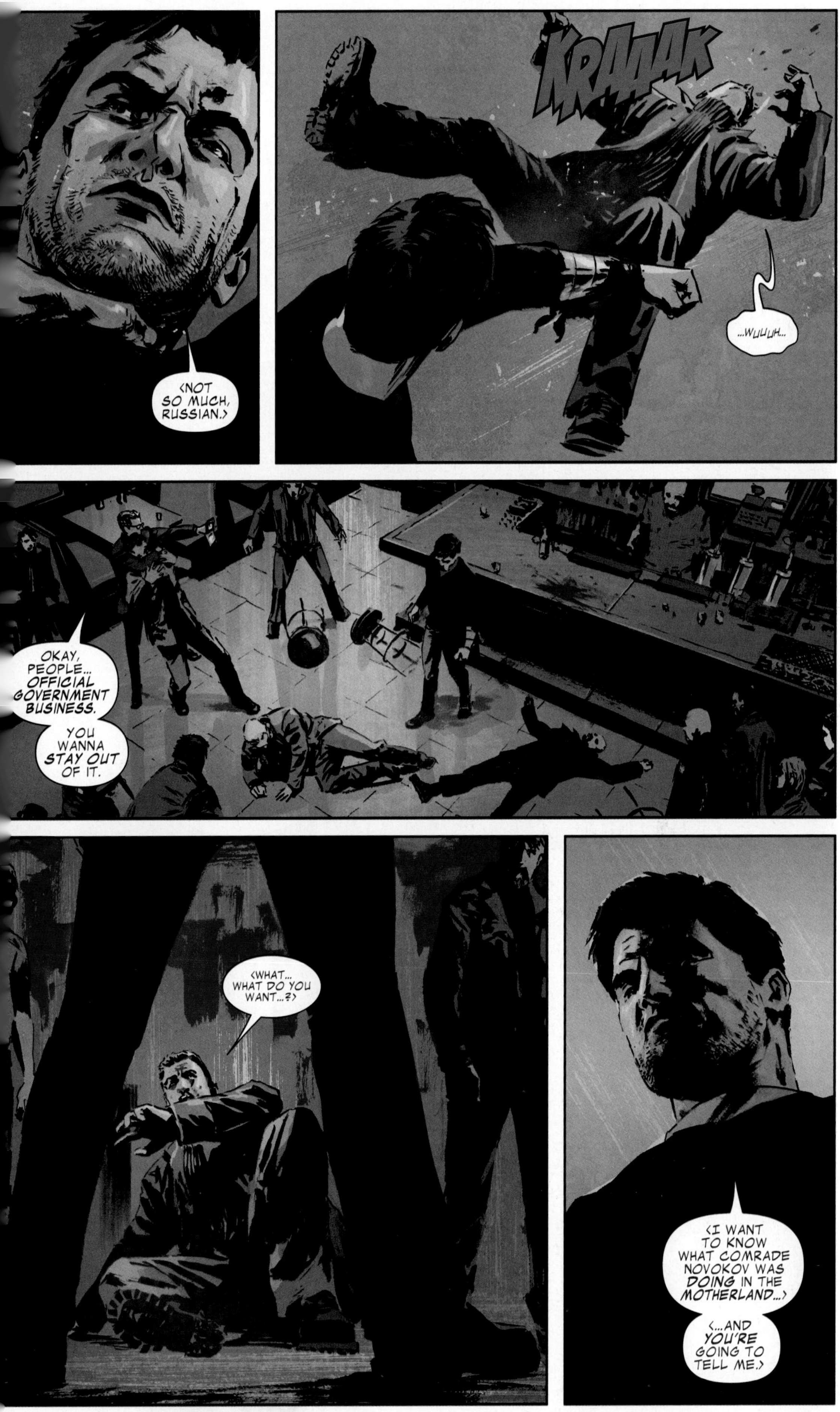

<NOT SO MUCH, RUSSIAN.>
KRAAAK
...WUUUH...
OKAY, PEOPLE... OFFICIAL GOVERNMENT BUSINESS.
YOU WANNA STAY OUT OF IT.
<WHAT... WHAT DO YOU WANT...?>
<I WANT TO KNOW WHAT COMRADE NOVOKOV WAS DOING IN THE MOTHERLAND...>
<...AND YOU'RE GOING TO TELL ME.>

ALLEN, JUST...HOLD ON...

I DON'T WANNA *HEAR IT*, CAITLIN...

OUR *LEAD* HAS THREE BROKEN RIBS *AND A FRACTURED PELVIS*...

AND HER *UNDERSTUDY* SUDDENLY HAS THE FRIGGING *SWINE FLU*!

DO YOU *UNDERSTAND* HOW SCREWED WE ARE?!

I KNOW, THAT'S WHY I SET UP THIS--

WE HAVE A *PRIVATE DRESS REHEARSAL* IN TWO DAYS!

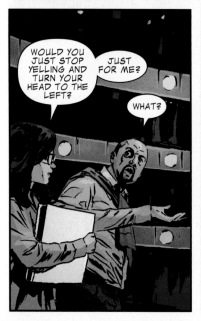

WOULD YOU JUST STOP YELLING AND TURN YOUR HEAD TO THE LEFT?

JUST FOR ME?

WHAT?

...MY GOD...

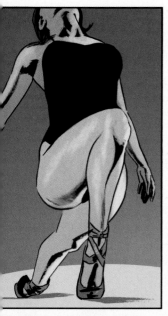

I TOLD YOU I'D FOUND SOMEBODY EXTRAORDINARY.

CAITLIN, YOU'RE AMAZING.

WHAT'S HER NAME?

NATALIA.

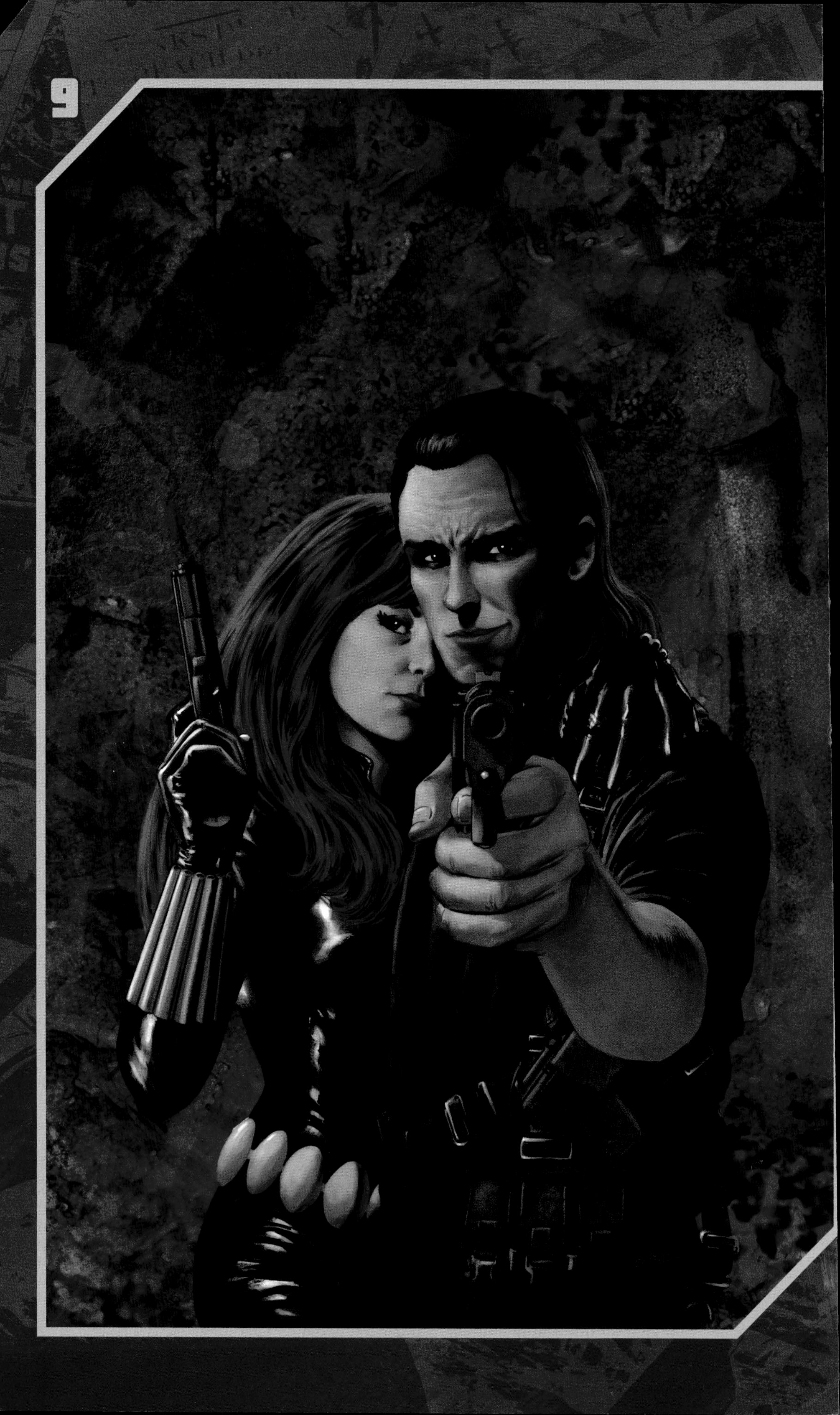
9

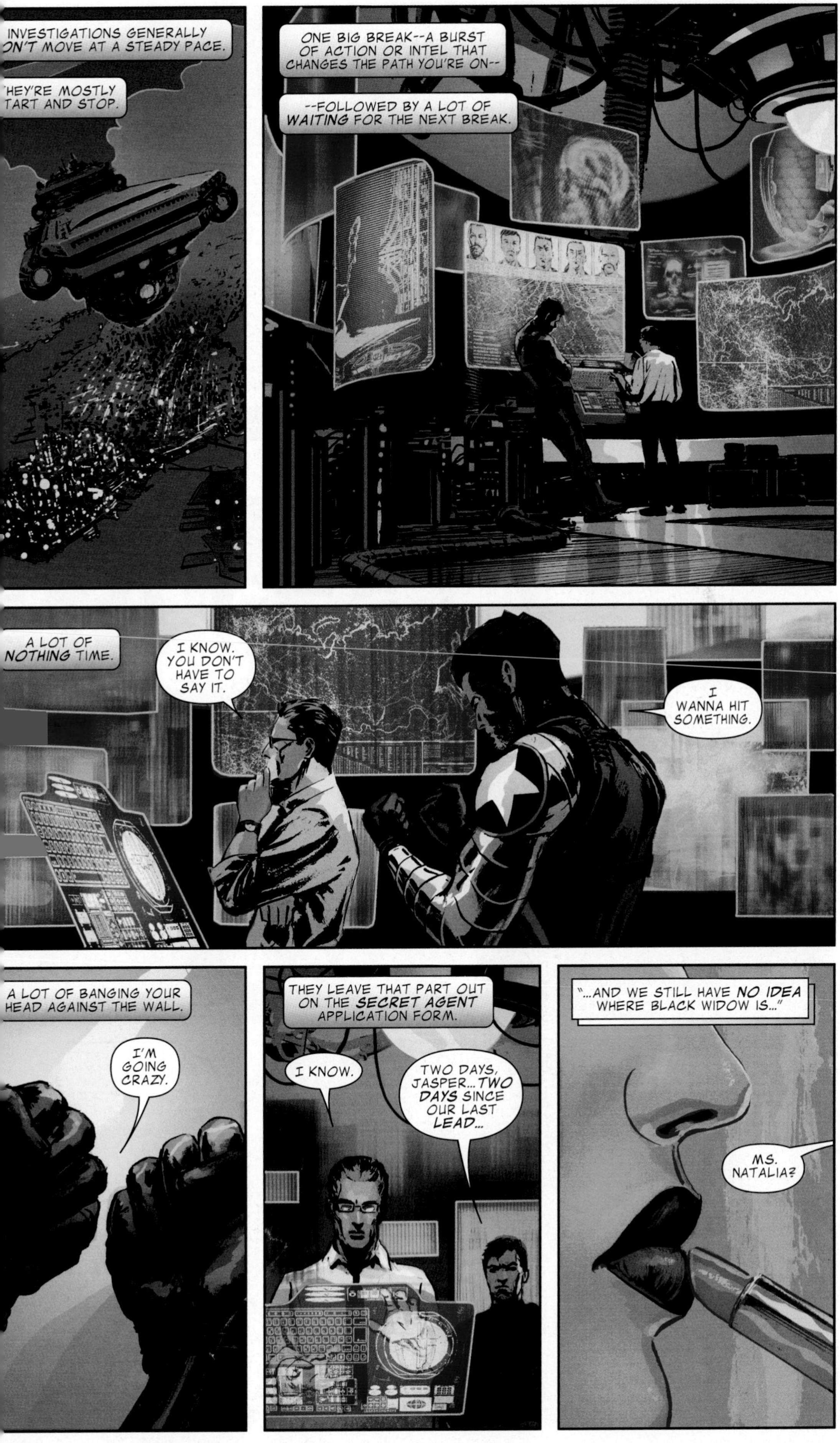

INVESTIGATIONS GENERALLY
ON'T MOVE AT A STEADY PACE.
HEY'RE MOSTLY
TART AND STOP.
ONE BIG BREAK--A BURST OF ACTION OR INTEL THAT CHANGES THE PATH YOU'RE ON--
--FOLLOWED BY A LOT OF WAITING FOR THE NEXT BREAK.
A LOT OF NOTHING TIME.
I KNOW. YOU DON'T HAVE TO SAY IT.
I WANNA HIT SOMETHING.
A LOT OF BANGING YOUR HEAD AGAINST THE WALL.
I'M GOING CRAZY.
THEY LEAVE THAT PART OUT ON THE SECRET AGENT APPLICATION FORM.
I KNOW.
TWO DAYS, JASPER... TWO DAYS SINCE OUR LAST LEAD...
"...AND WE STILL HAVE NO IDEA WHERE BLACK WIDOW IS..."
MS. NATALIA?

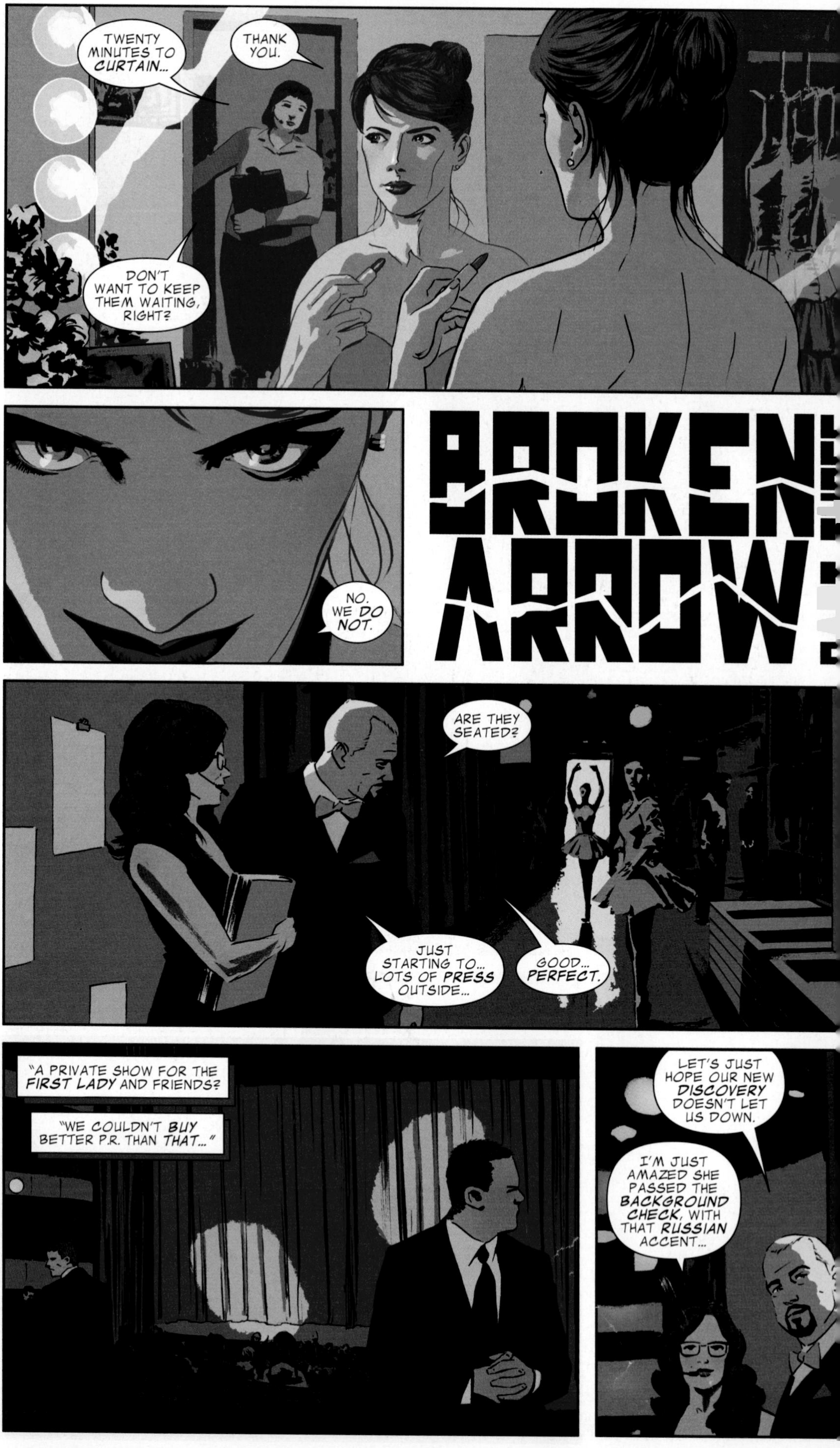
TWENTY MINUTES TO CURTAIN...
THANK YOU.
DON'T WANT TO KEEP THEM WAITING, RIGHT?
NO. WE DO NOT.
BROKEN ARROW
ARE THEY SEATED?
JUST STARTING TO... LOTS OF PRESS OUTSIDE...
GOOD... PERFECT.
"A PRIVATE SHOW FOR THE FIRST LADY AND FRIENDS?
"WE COULDN'T BUY BETTER P.R. THAN THAT..."
LET'S JUST HOPE OUR NEW DISCOVERY DOESN'T LET US DOWN.
I'M JUST AMAZED SHE PASSED THE BACKGROUND CHECK, WITH THAT RUSSIAN ACCENT...

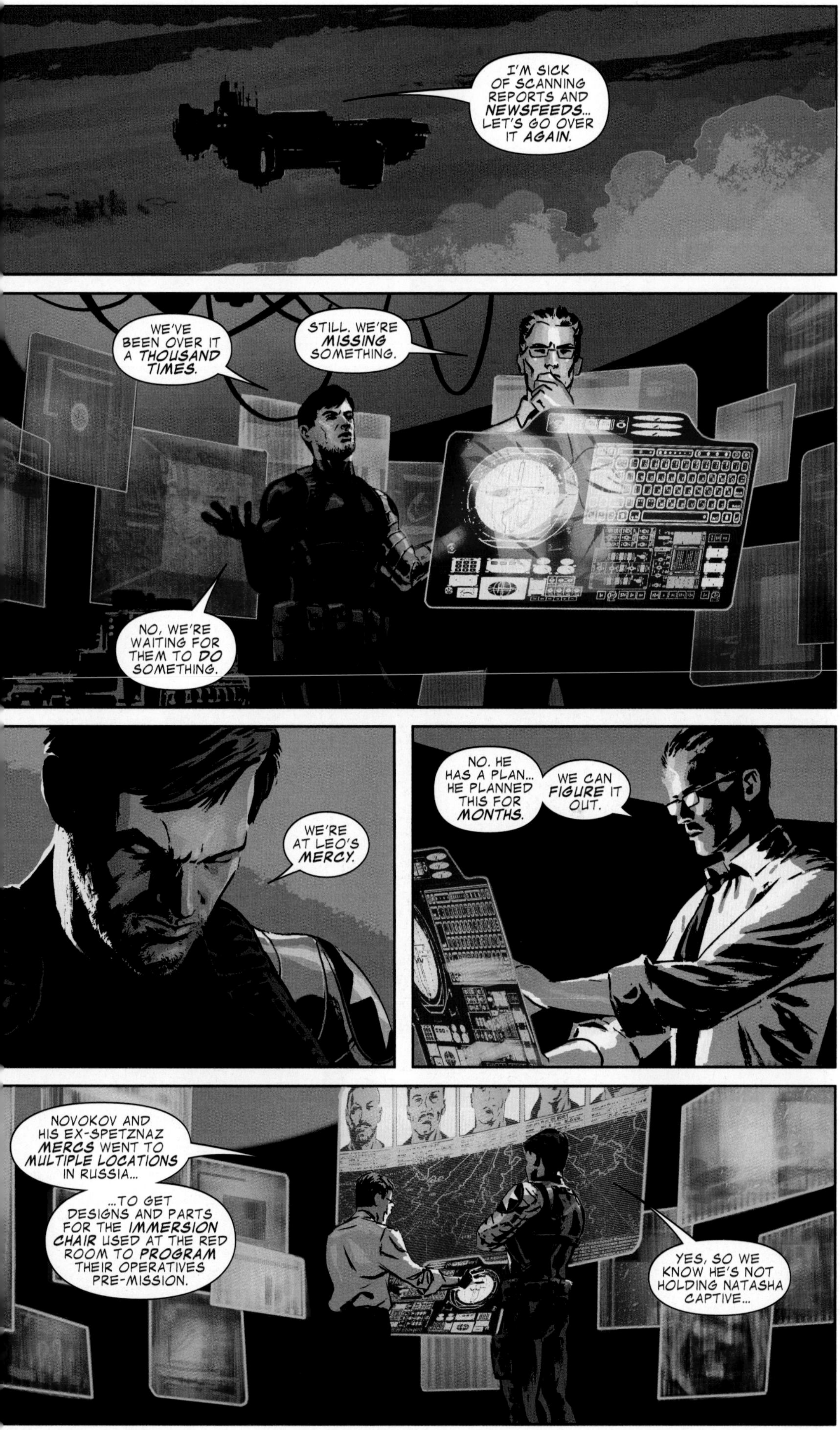
I'M SICK OF SCANNING REPORTS AND NEWSFEEDS... LET'S GO OVER IT AGAIN.
WE'VE BEEN OVER IT A THOUSAND TIMES.
STILL. WE'RE MISSING SOMETHING.
NO, WE'RE WAITING FOR THEM TO DO SOMETHING.
WE'RE AT LEO'S MERCY.
NO. HE HAS A PLAN... HE PLANNED THIS FOR MONTHS.
WE CAN FIGURE IT OUT.
NOVOKOV AND HIS EX-SPETZNAZ MERCS WENT TO MULTIPLE LOCATIONS IN RUSSIA...
...TO GET DESIGNS AND PARTS FOR THE IMMERSION CHAIR USED AT THE RED ROOM TO PROGRAM THEIR OPERATIVES PRE-MISSION.
YES, SO WE KNOW HE'S NOT HOLDING NATASHA CAPTIVE...

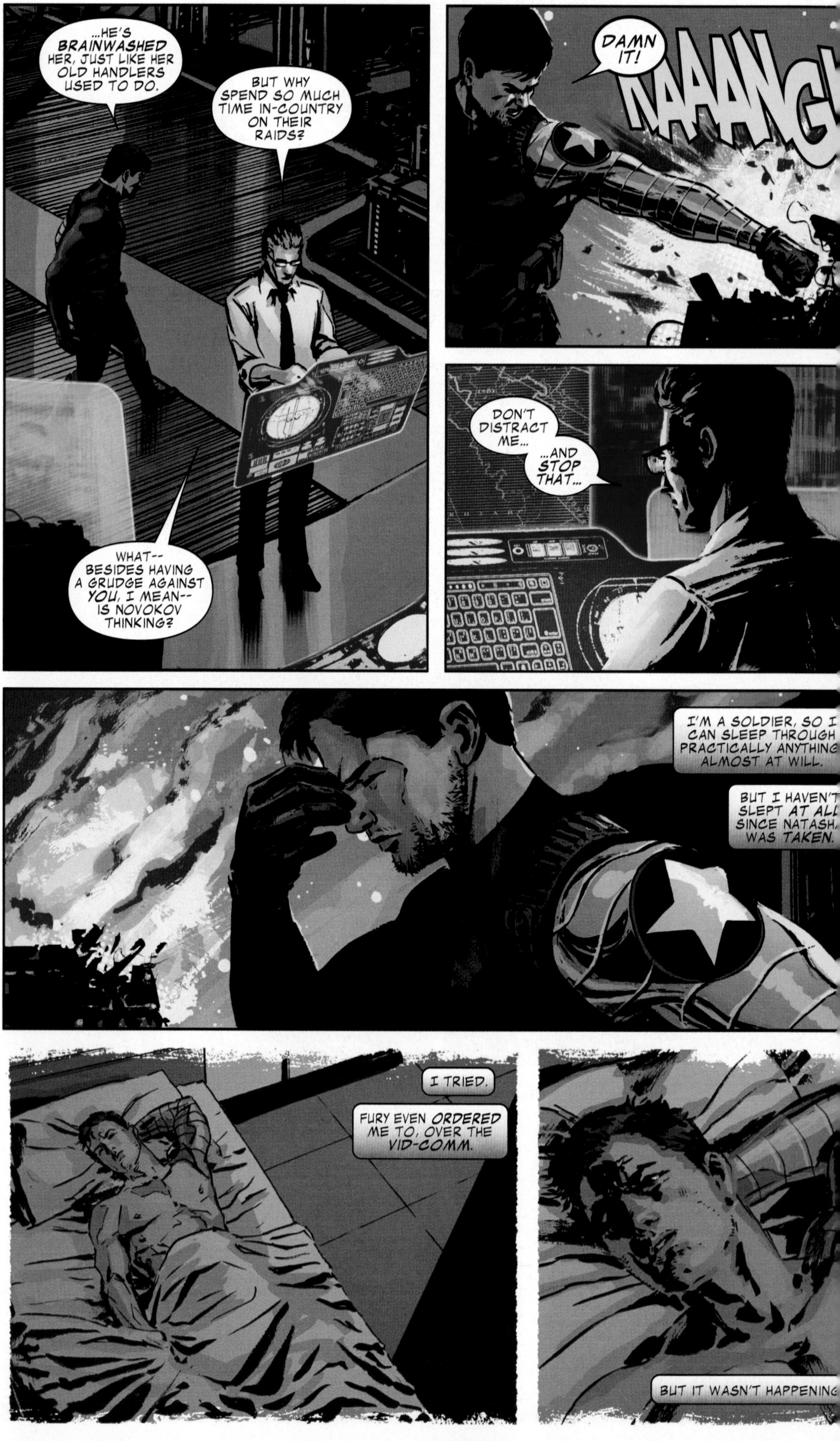
...HE'S BRAINWASHED HER, JUST LIKE HER OLD HANDLERS USED TO DO.
BUT WHY SPEND SO MUCH TIME IN-COUNTRY ON THEIR RAIDS?
WHAT-- BESIDES HAVING A GRUDGE AGAINST YOU, I MEAN-- IS NOVOKOV THINKING?
DAMN IT!
DON'T DISTRACT ME...
...AND STOP THAT...
I'M A SOLDIER, SO I CAN SLEEP THROUGH PRACTICALLY ANYTHING ALMOST AT WILL.
BUT I HAVEN'T SLEPT AT ALL SINCE NATASHA WAS TAKEN.
I TRIED.
FURY EVEN ORDERED ME TO, OVER THE VID-COMM.
BUT IT WASN'T HAPPENING.

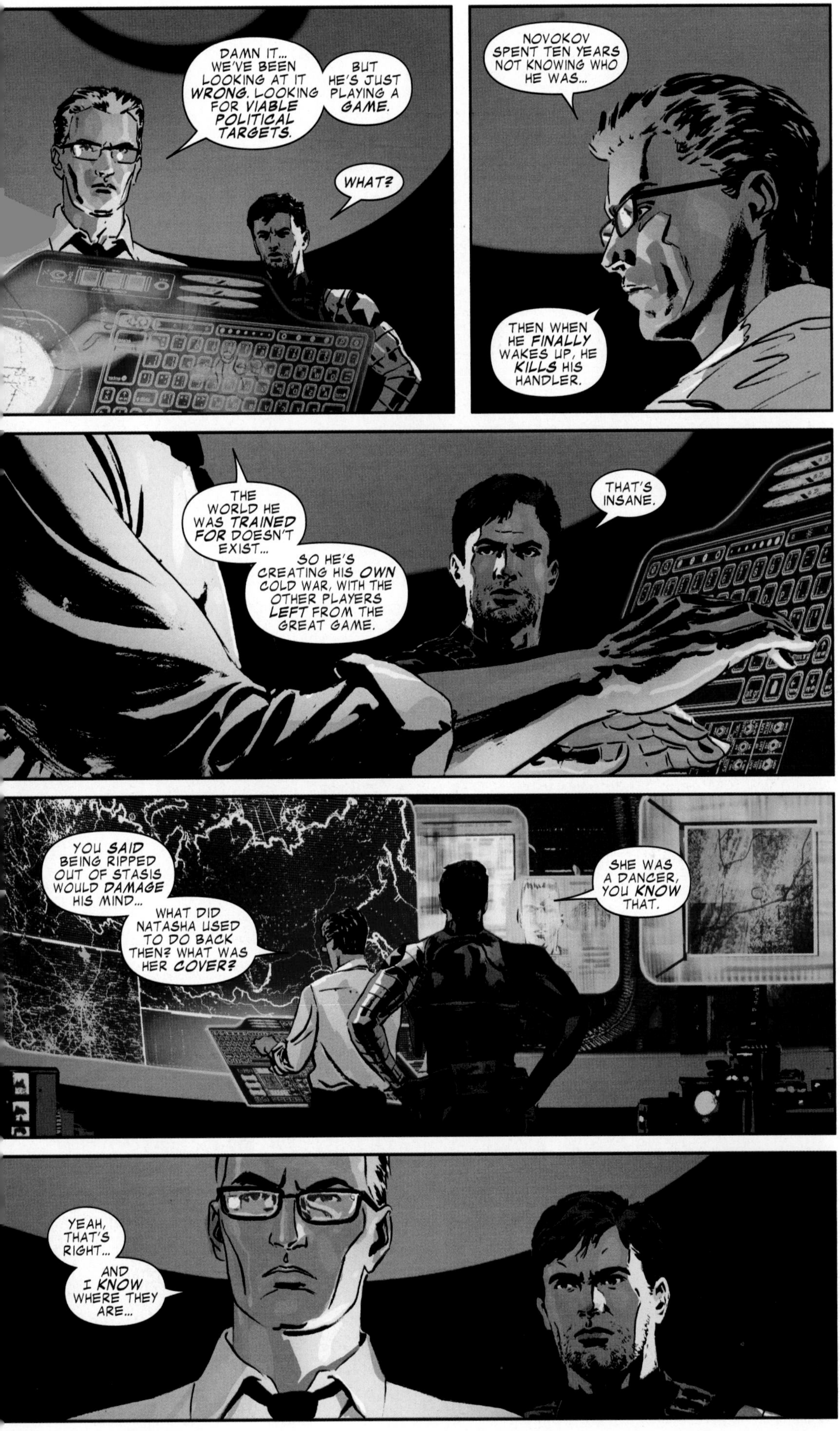
DAMN IT... WE'VE BEEN LOOKING AT IT WRONG. LOOKING FOR VIABLE POLITICAL TARGETS.
BUT HE'S JUST PLAYING A GAME.
WHAT?
NOVOKOV SPENT TEN YEARS NOT KNOWING WHO HE WAS...
THEN WHEN HE FINALLY WAKES UP, HE KILLS HIS HANDLER.
THE WORLD HE WAS TRAINED FOR DOESN'T EXIST...
SO HE'S CREATING HIS OWN COLD WAR, WITH THE OTHER PLAYERS LEFT FROM THE GREAT GAME.
THAT'S INSANE.
YOU SAID BEING RIPPED OUT OF STASIS WOULD DAMAGE HIS MIND...
WHAT DID NATASHA USED TO DO BACK THEN? WHAT WAS HER COVER?
SHE WAS A DANCER, YOU KNOW THAT.
YEAH, THAT'S RIGHT...
AND I KNOW WHERE THEY ARE...

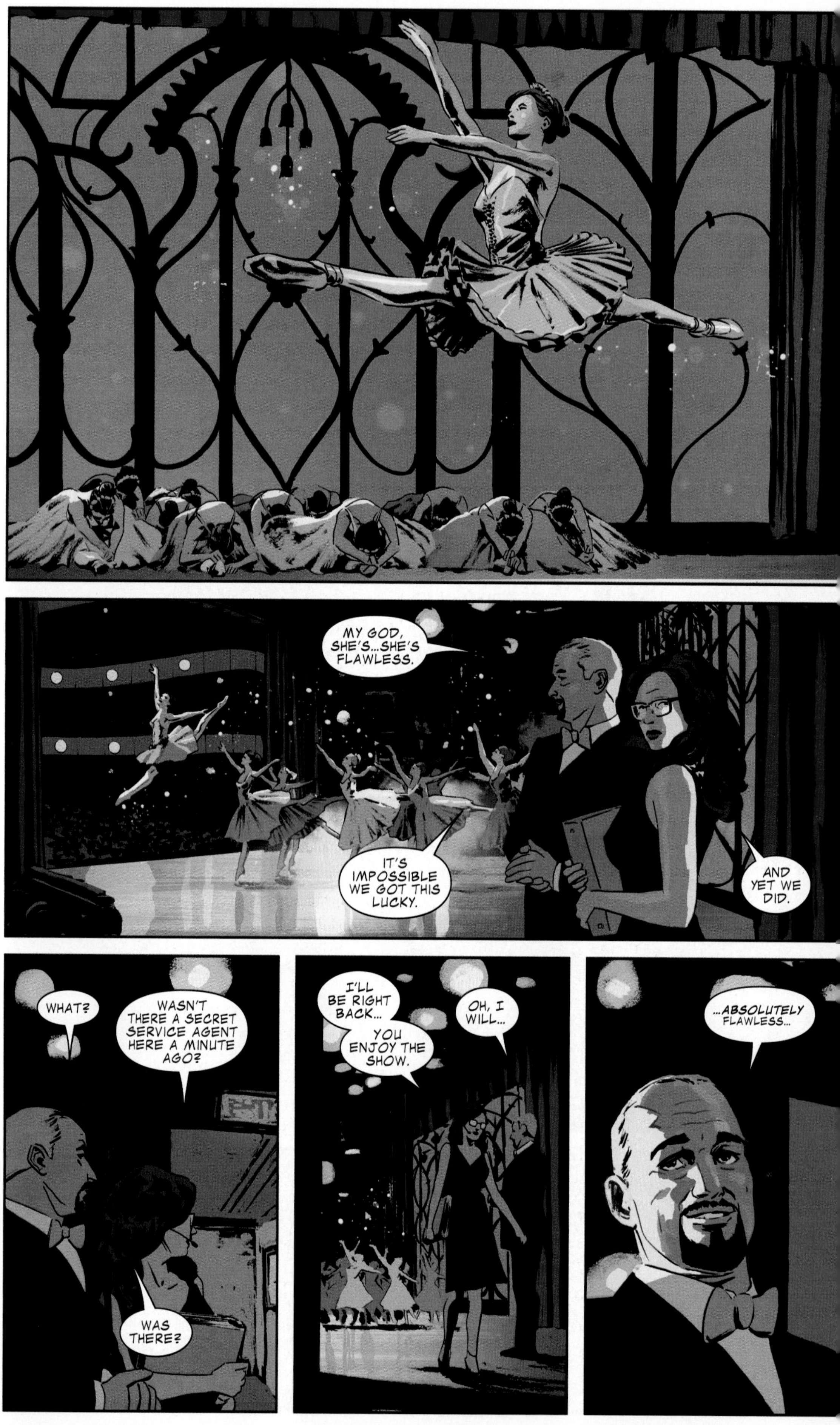

MY GOD, SHE'S...SHE'S FLAWLESS.
IT'S IMPOSSIBLE WE GOT THIS LUCKY.
AND YET WE DID.
WHAT?
WASN'T THERE A SECRET SERVICE AGENT HERE A MINUTE AGO?
WAS THERE?
I'LL BE RIGHT BACK...
YOU ENJOY THE SHOW.
OH, I WILL...
...ABSOLUTELY FLAWLESS...

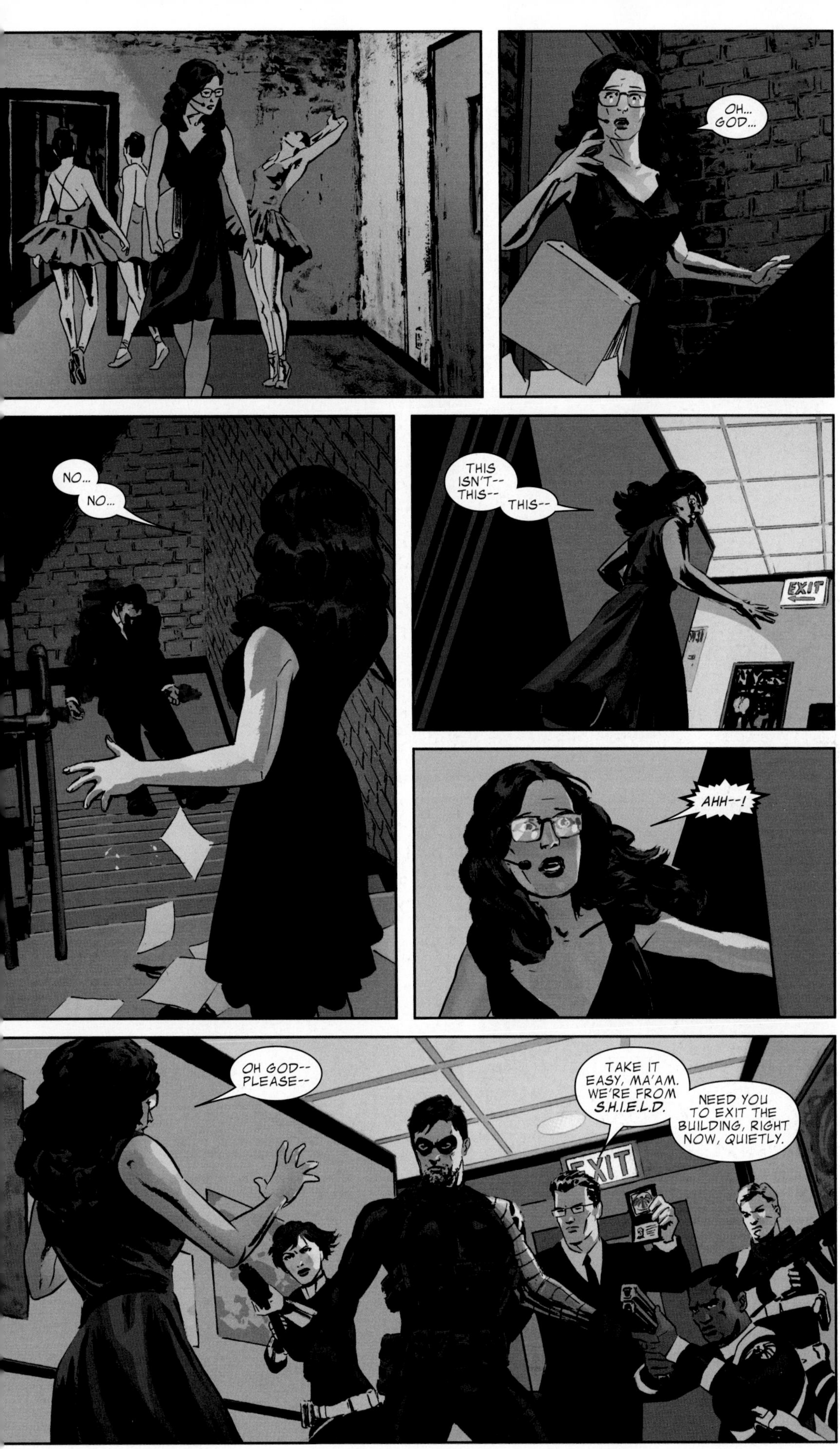

OH... GOD...
NO... NO...
THIS ISN'T-- THIS--
THIS--
EXIT
AHH--!
OH GOD-- PLEASE--
TAKE IT EASY, MA'AM. WE'RE FROM S.H.I.E.L.D.
NEED YOU TO EXIT THE BUILDING, RIGHT NOW, QUIETLY.
EXIT

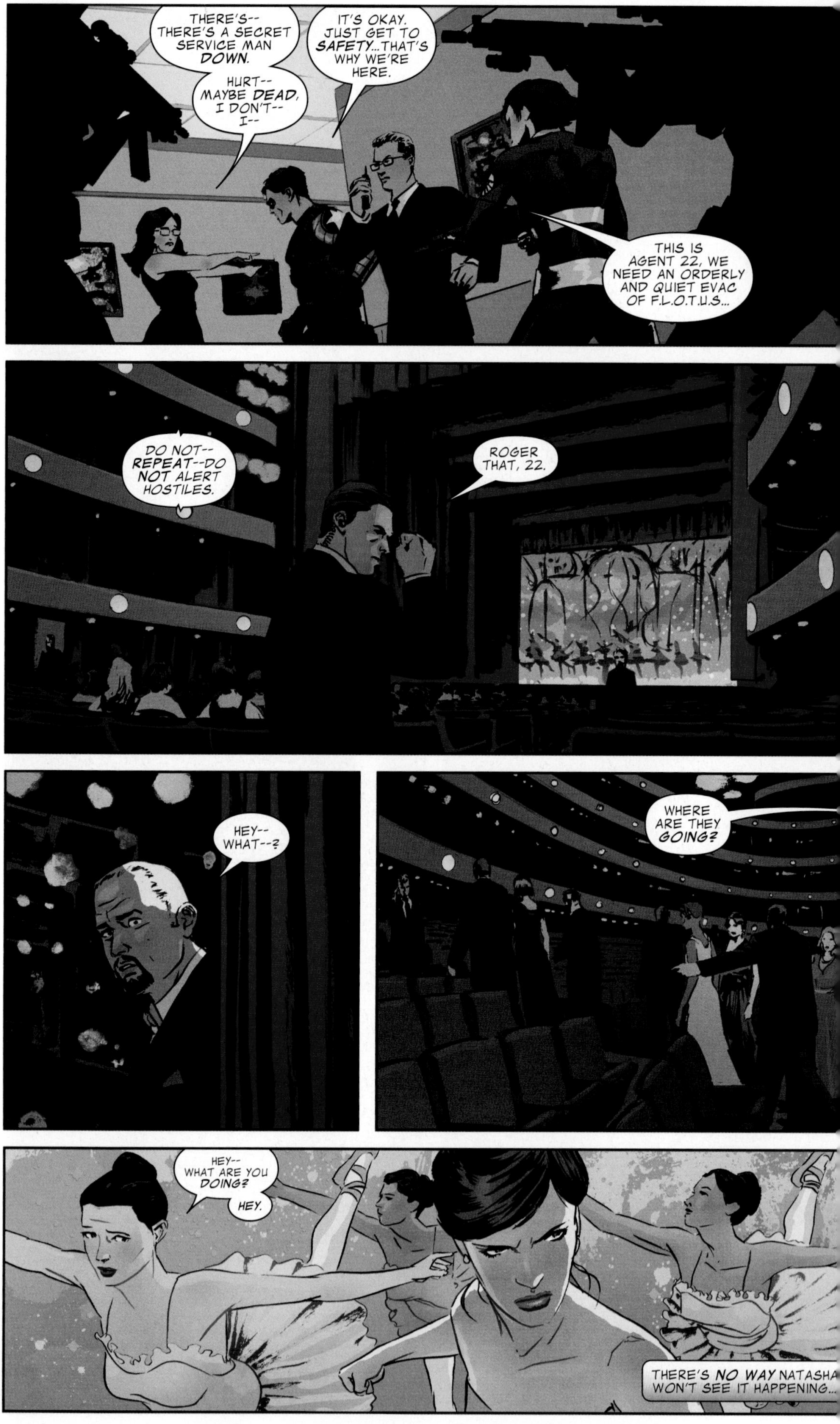
THERE'S-- THERE'S A SECRET SERVICE MAN DOWN.
HURT-- MAYBE DEAD, I DON'T-- I--
IT'S OKAY. JUST GET TO SAFETY...THAT'S WHY WE'RE HERE.
THIS IS AGENT 22, WE NEED AN ORDERLY AND QUIET EVAC OF F.L.O.T.U.S...
DO NOT-- REPEAT--DO NOT ALERT HOSTILES.
ROGER THAT, 22.
HEY-- WHAT--?
WHERE ARE THEY GOING?
HEY-- WHAT ARE YOU DOING?
HEY.
THERE'S NO WAY NATASHA WON'T SEE IT HAPPENING...

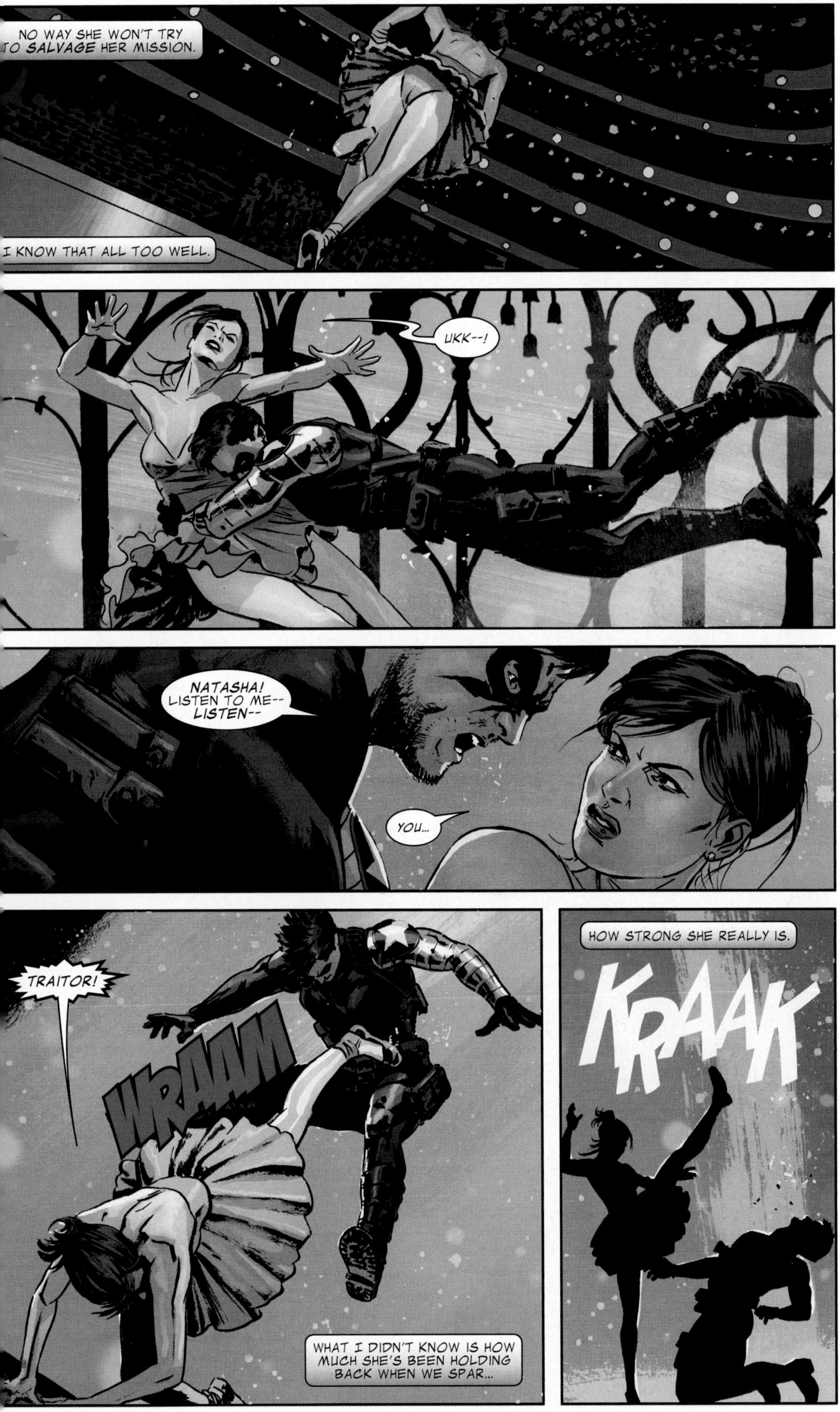
NO WAY SHE WON'T TRY TO SALVAGE HER MISSION.
I KNOW THAT ALL TOO WELL.
UKK--!
NATASHA! LISTEN TO ME-- LISTEN--
YOU...
TRAITOR!
WRAAM
WHAT I DIDN'T KNOW IS HOW MUCH SHE'S BEEN HOLDING BACK WHEN WE SPAR...
HOW STRONG SHE REALLY IS.
KRAAK

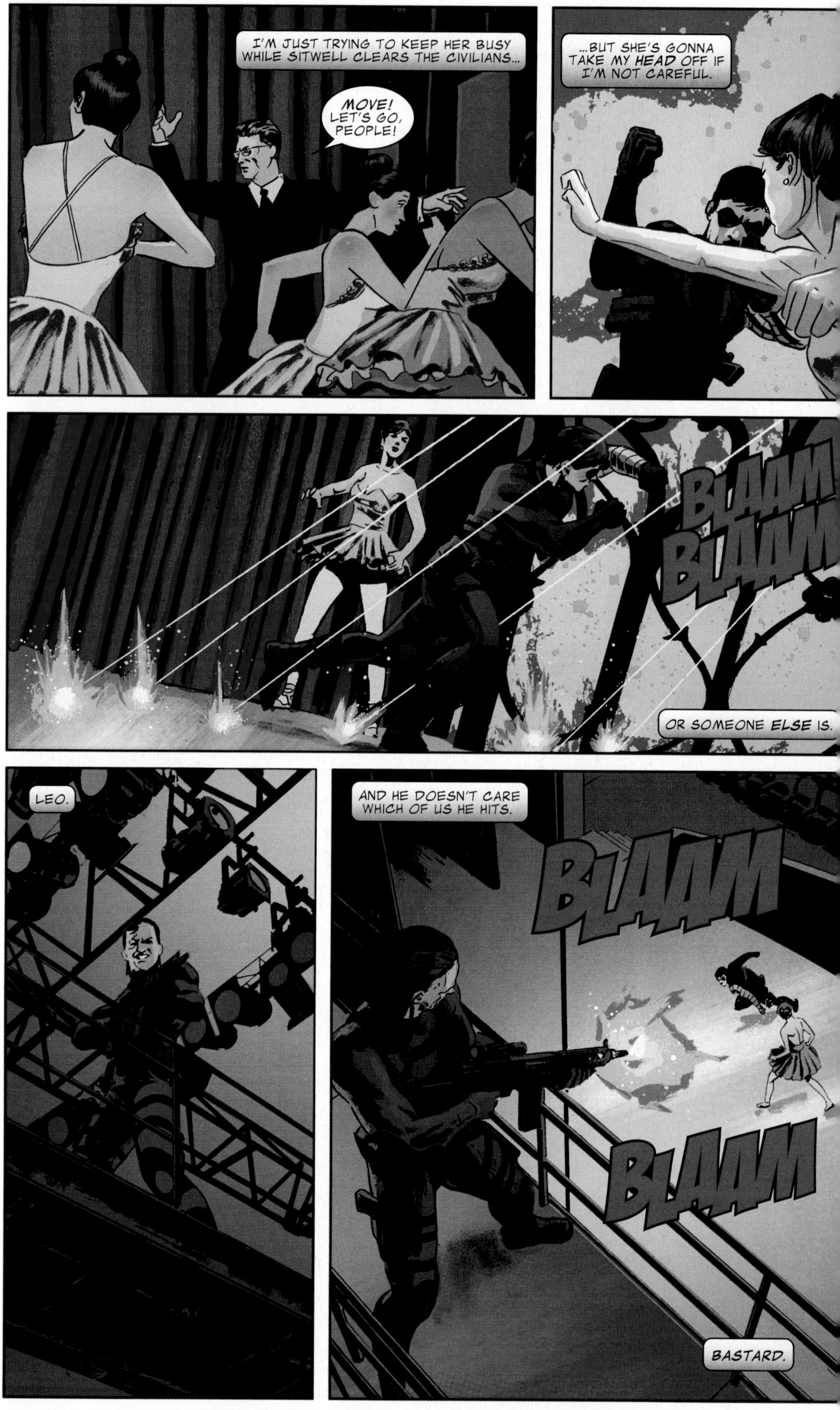
I'M JUST TRYING TO KEEP HER BUSY WHILE SITWELL CLEARS THE CIVILIANS...
MOVE! LET'S GO, PEOPLE!
...BUT SHE'S GONNA TAKE MY HEAD OFF IF I'M NOT CAREFUL.
BLAAAM
BLAAAM
OR SOMEONE ELSE IS.
LEO.
AND HE DOESN'T CARE WHICH OF US HE HITS.
BLAAAM
BLAAAM
BASTARD.

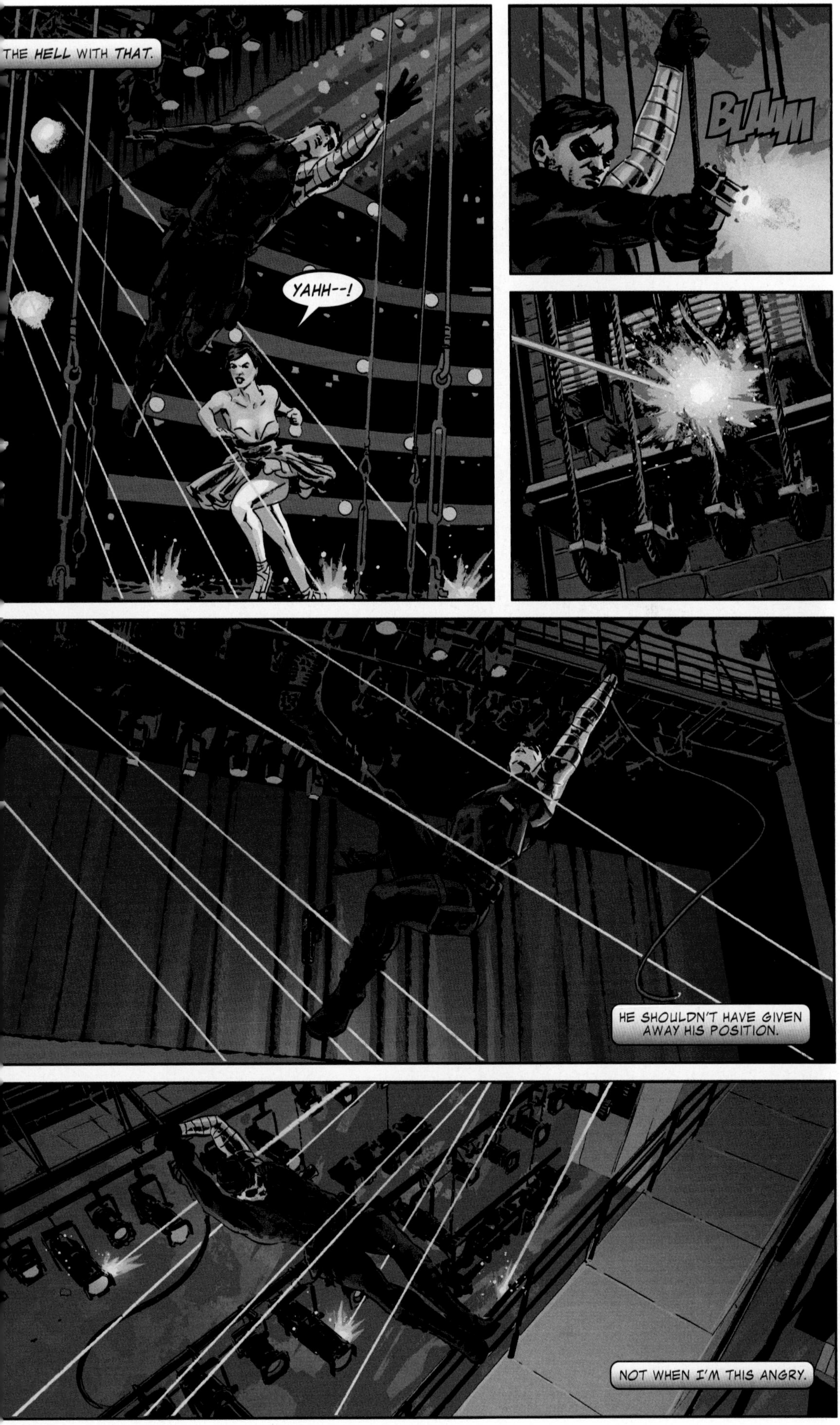
THE HELL WITH THAT.
YAHH--!
BLAAM
HE SHOULDN'T HAVE GIVEN AWAY HIS POSITION.
NOT WHEN I'M THIS ANGRY.

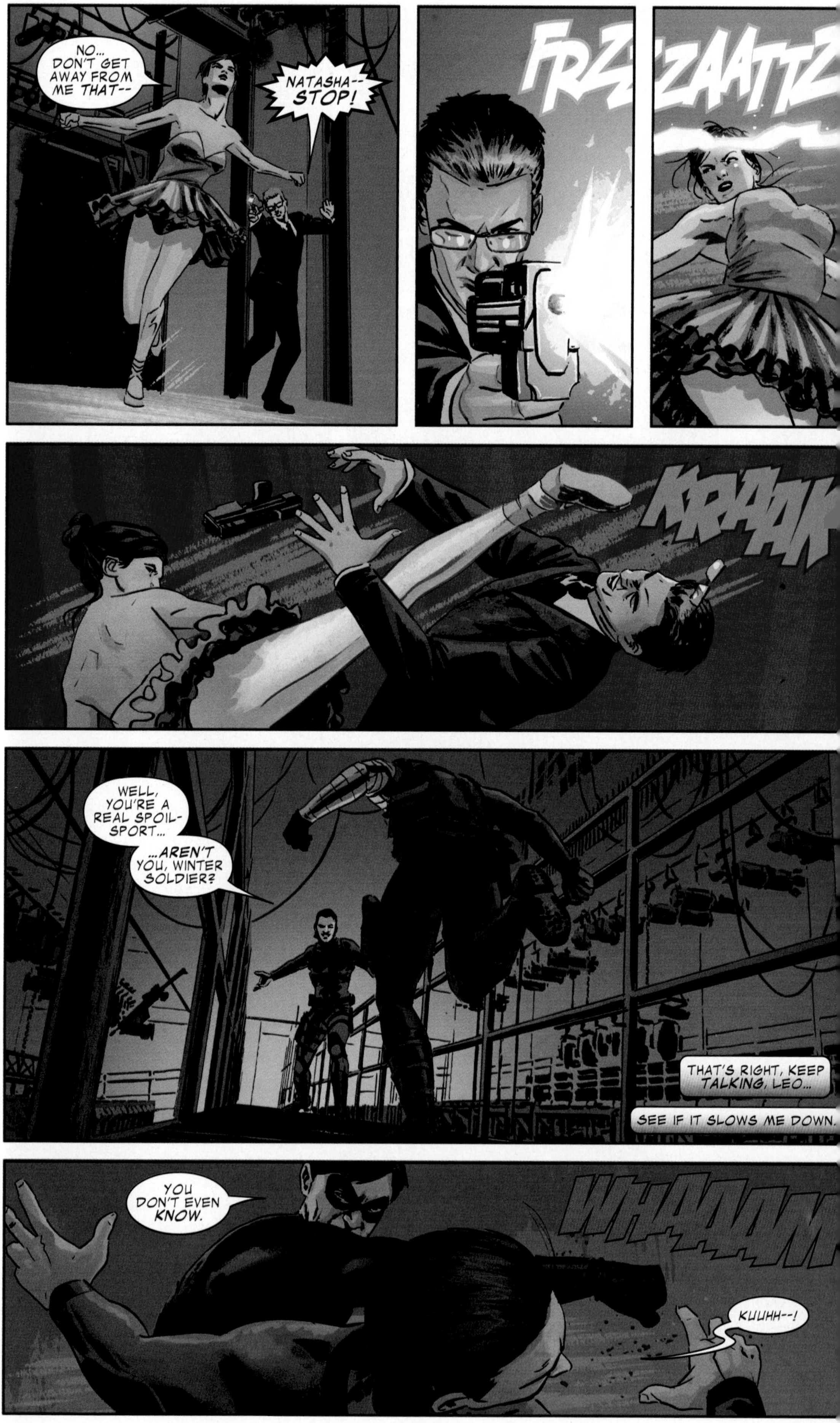

NO... DON'T GET AWAY FROM ME THAT--
NATASHA-- STOP!
FRZZZZAATTZ
KRAAAK
WELL, YOU'RE A REAL SPOIL-SPORT...
...AREN'T YOU, WINTER SOLDIER?
THAT'S RIGHT, KEEP TALKING, LEO...
SEE IF IT SLOWS ME DOWN.
YOU DON'T EVEN KNOW.
WHAAAM
KUUHH--!

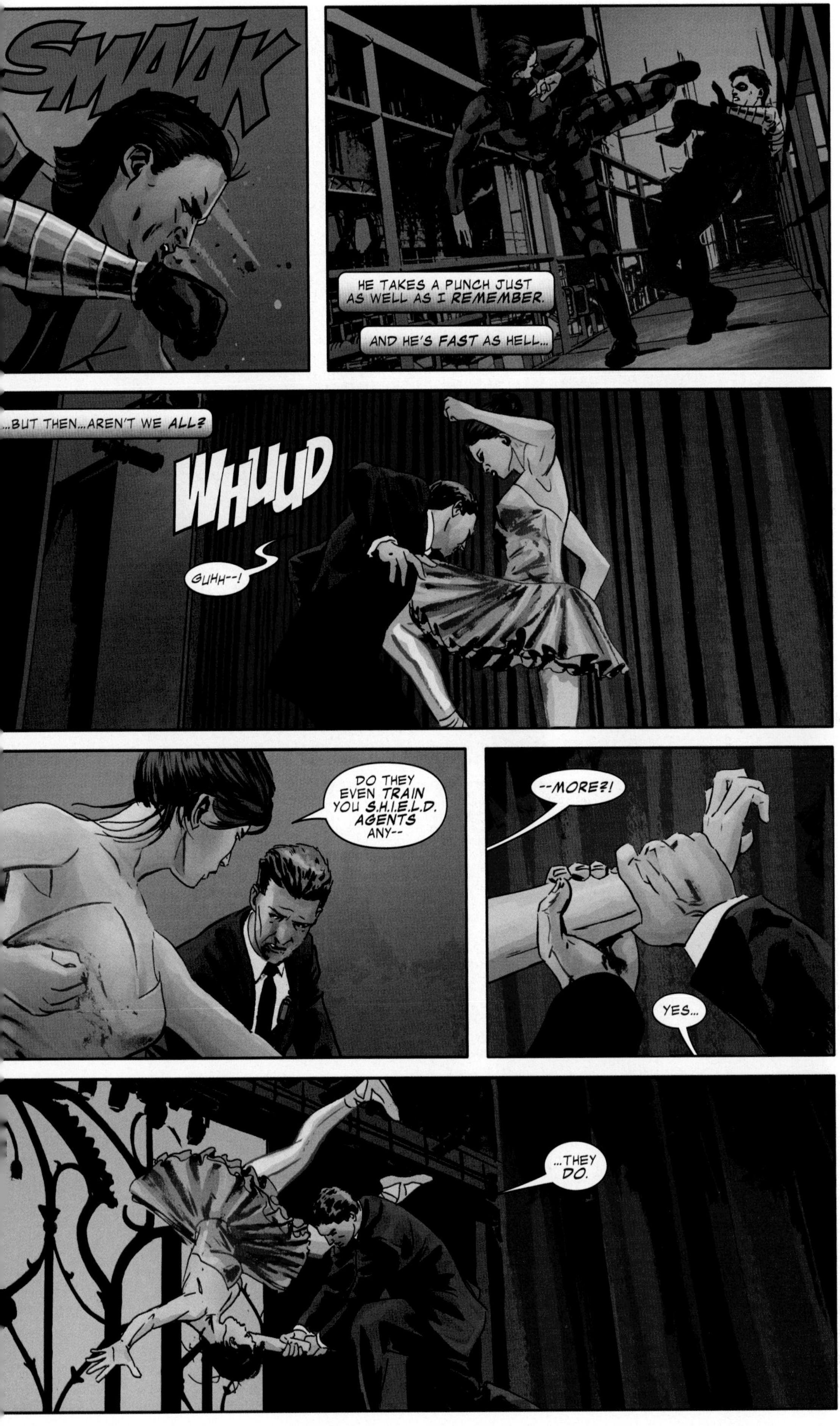
SMAAK
HE TAKES A PUNCH JUST AS WELL AS I REMEMBER.
AND HE'S FAST AS HELL...
...BUT THEN...AREN'T WE ALL?
WHUUD
GUHH--!
DO THEY EVEN TRAIN YOU S.H.I.E.L.D. AGENTS ANY--
--MORE?!
YES...
...THEY DO.

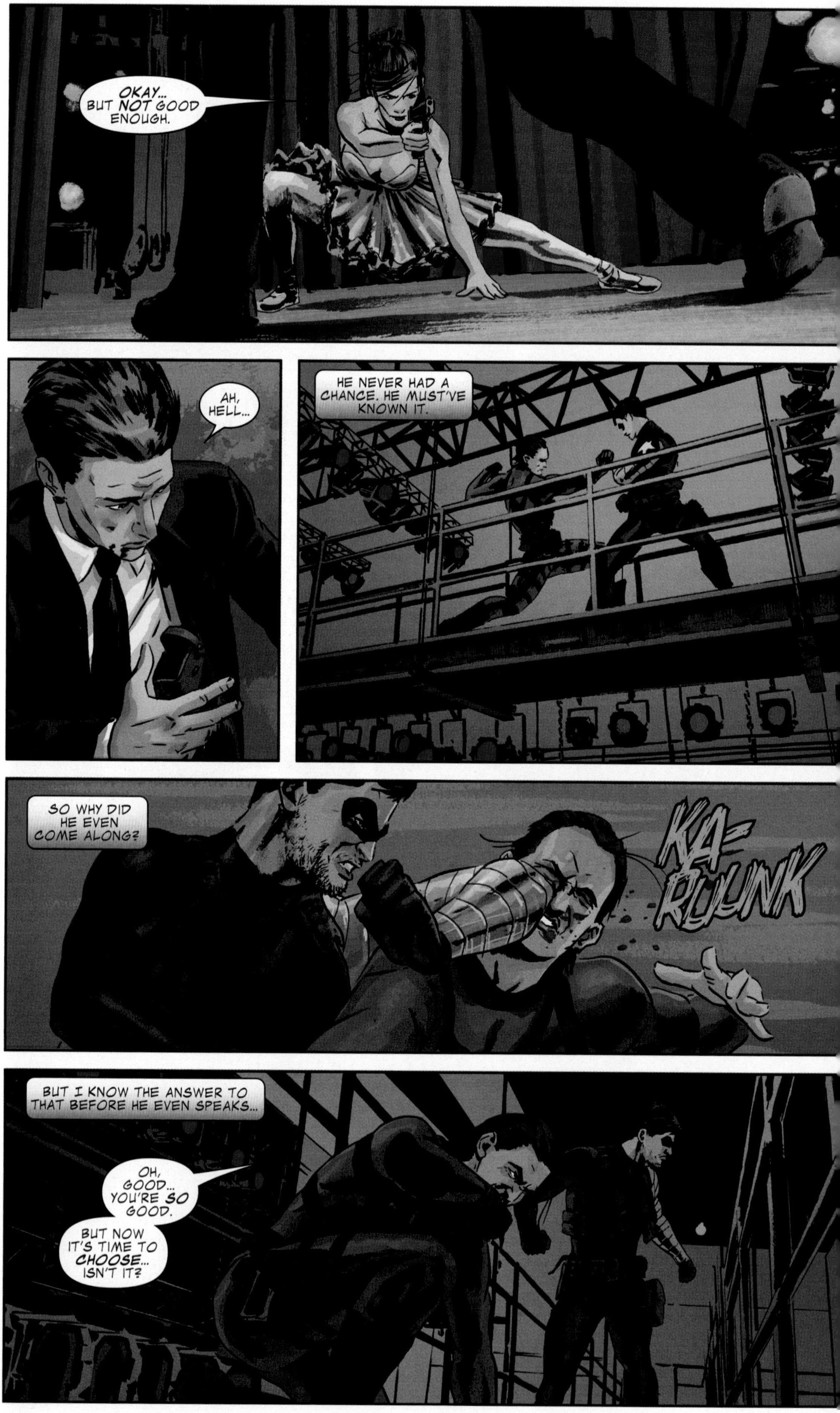
OKAY... BUT NOT GOOD ENOUGH.
AH, HELL...
HE NEVER HAD A CHANCE. HE MUST'VE KNOWN IT.
SO WHY DID HE EVEN COME ALONG?
KA-RUUNK
BUT I KNOW THE ANSWER TO THAT BEFORE HE EVEN SPEAKS...
OH, GOOD... YOU'RE SO GOOD.
BUT NOW IT'S TIME TO CHOOSE... ISN'T IT?

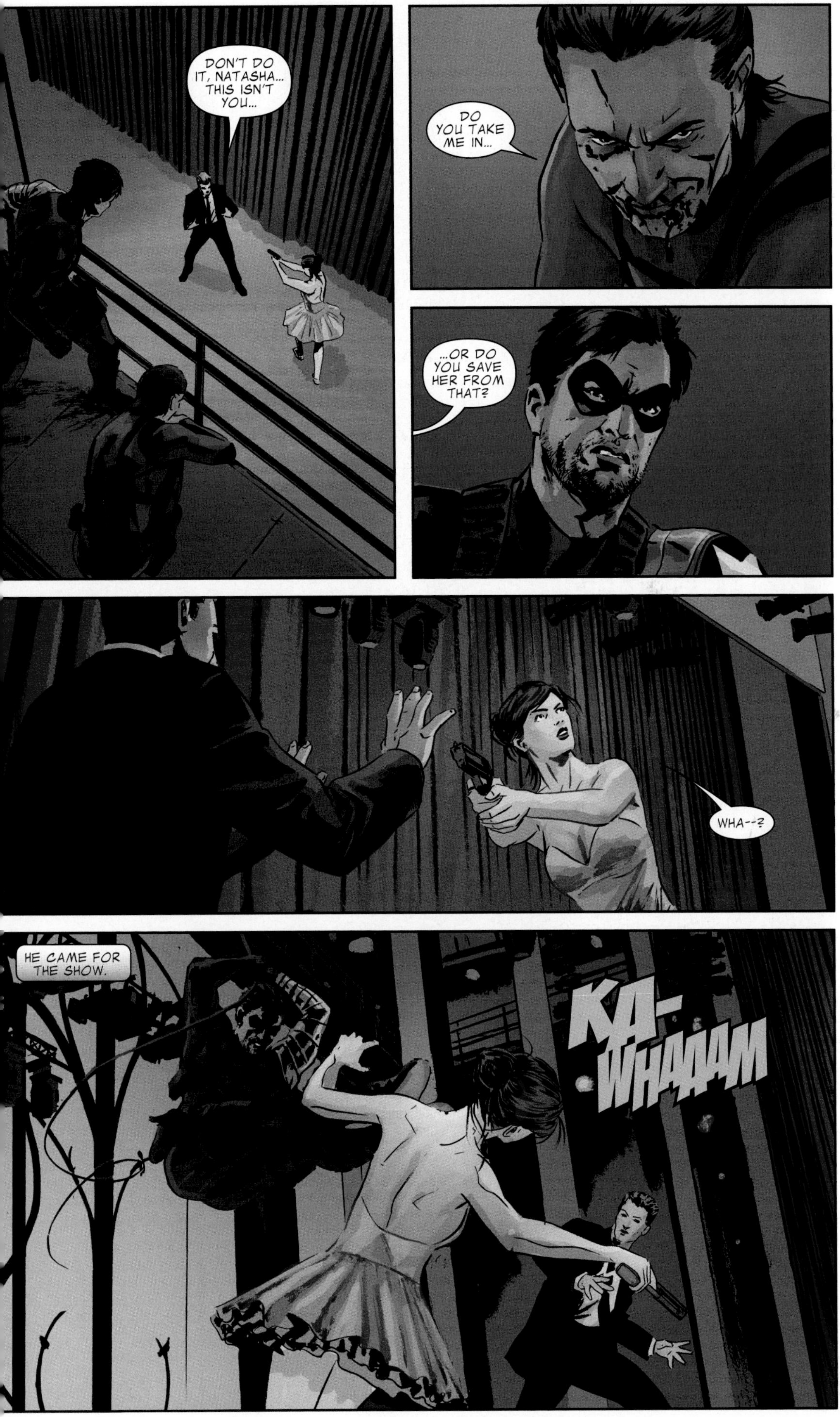
DON'T DO IT, NATASHA... THIS ISN'T YOU...
DO YOU TAKE ME IN...
...OR DO YOU SAVE HER FROM THAT?
WHA--?
HE CAME FOR THE SHOW.
KA-WHAAAM

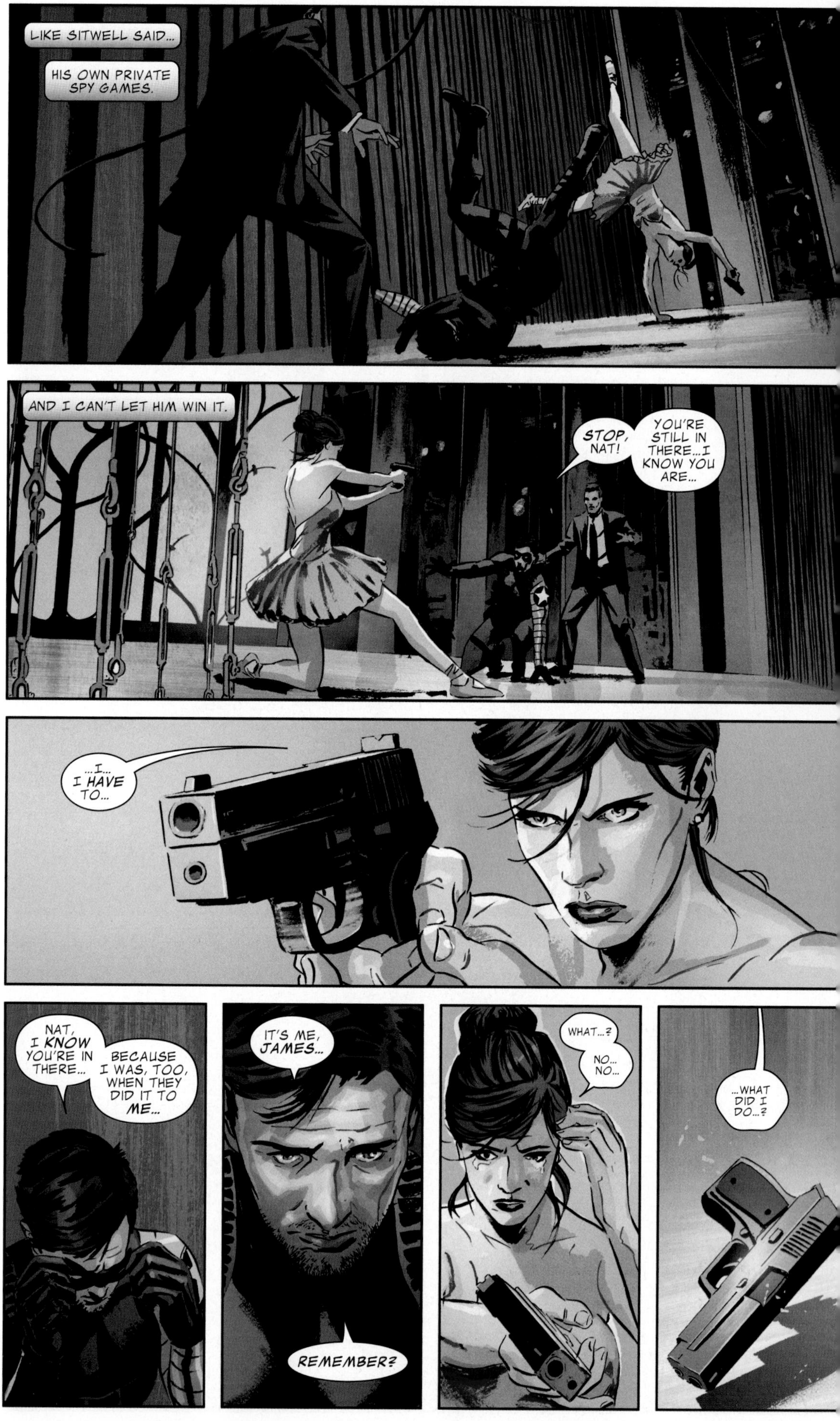
LIKE SITWELL SAID...
HIS OWN PRIVATE SPY GAMES.
AND I CAN'T LET HIM WIN IT.
STOP, NAT!
YOU'RE STILL IN THERE...I KNOW YOU ARE...
...I... I HAVE TO...
NAT, I KNOW YOU'RE IN THERE...
BECAUSE I WAS, TOO, WHEN THEY DID IT TO ME...
IT'S ME, JAMES...
REMEMBER?
WHAT...?
NO... NO...
...WHAT DID I DO...?

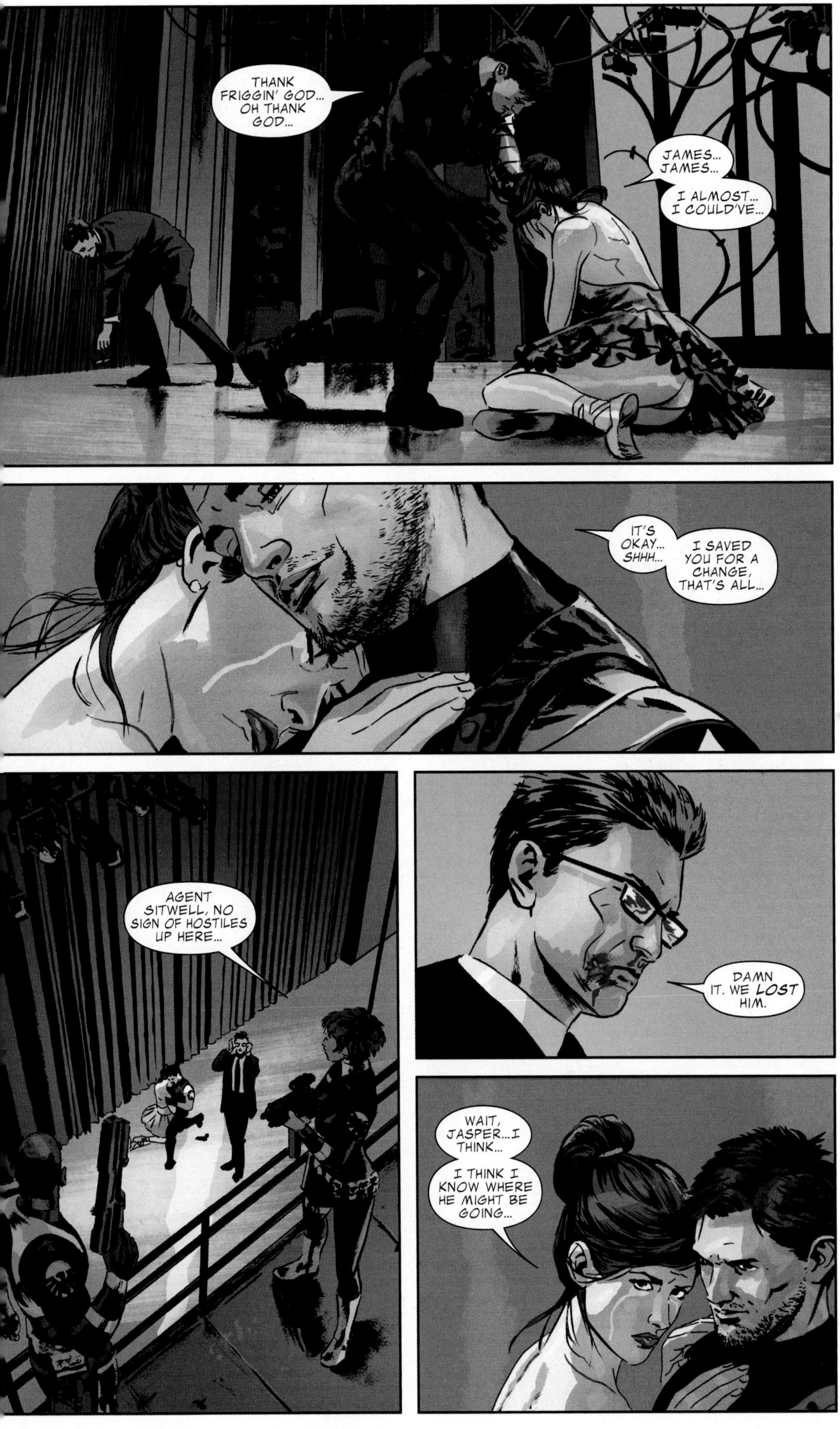
THANK FRIGGIN' GOD... OH THANK GOD...
JAMES... JAMES...
I ALMOST... I COULD'VE...
IT'S OKAY... SHHH...
I SAVED YOU FOR A CHANGE, THAT'S ALL...
AGENT SITWELL, NO SIGN OF HOSTILES UP HERE...
DAMN IT. WE LOST HIM.
WAIT, JASPER...I THINK...
I THINK I KNOW WHERE HE MIGHT BE GOING...

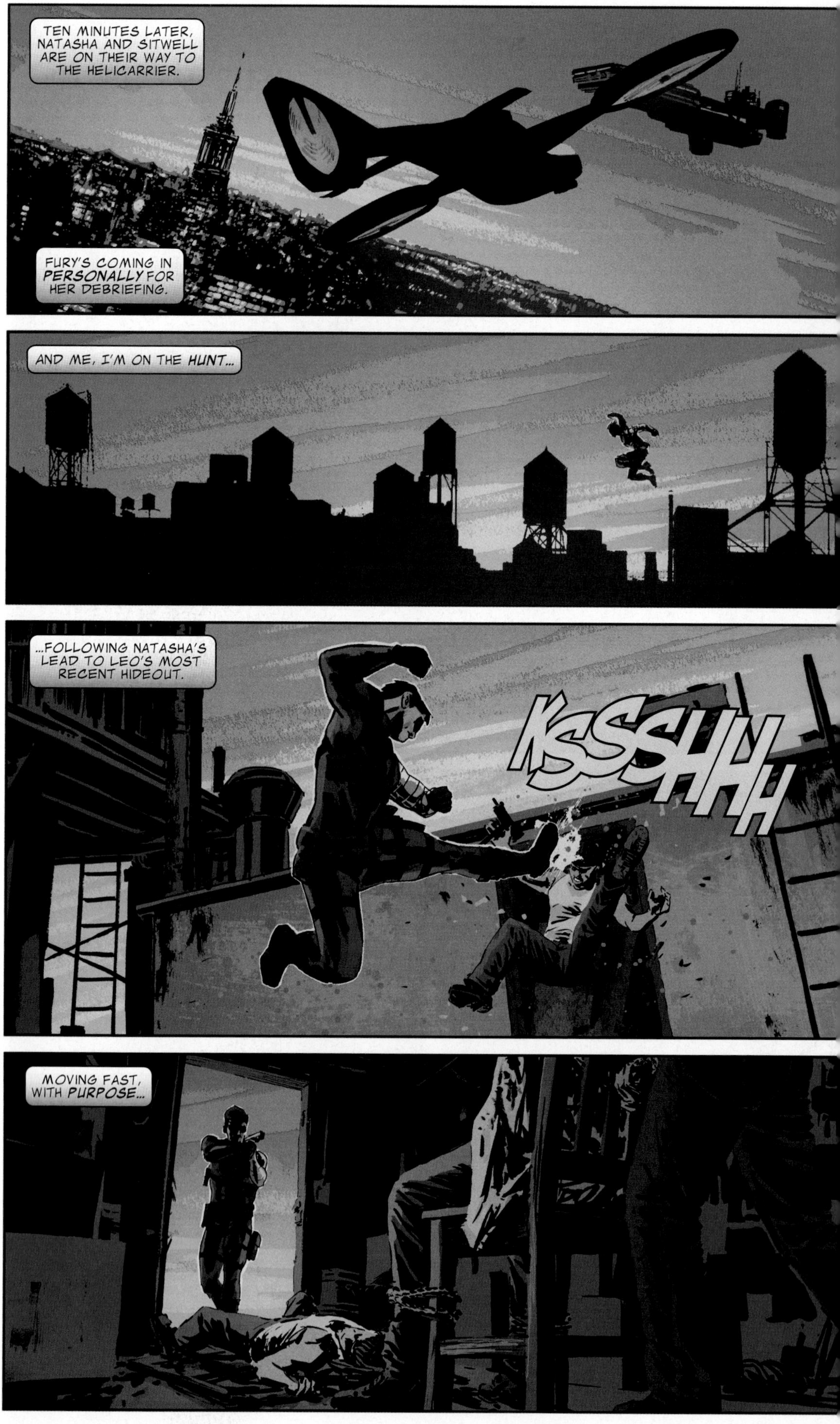
TEN MINUTES LATER, NATASHA AND SITWELL ARE ON THEIR WAY TO THE HELICARRIER.
FURY'S COMING IN *PERSONALLY* FOR HER DEBRIEFING.
AND ME, I'M ON THE *HUNT*...
...FOLLOWING NATASHA'S LEAD TO LEO'S MOST RECENT HIDEOUT.
KSSSHHH
MOVING FAST, WITH *PURPOSE*...

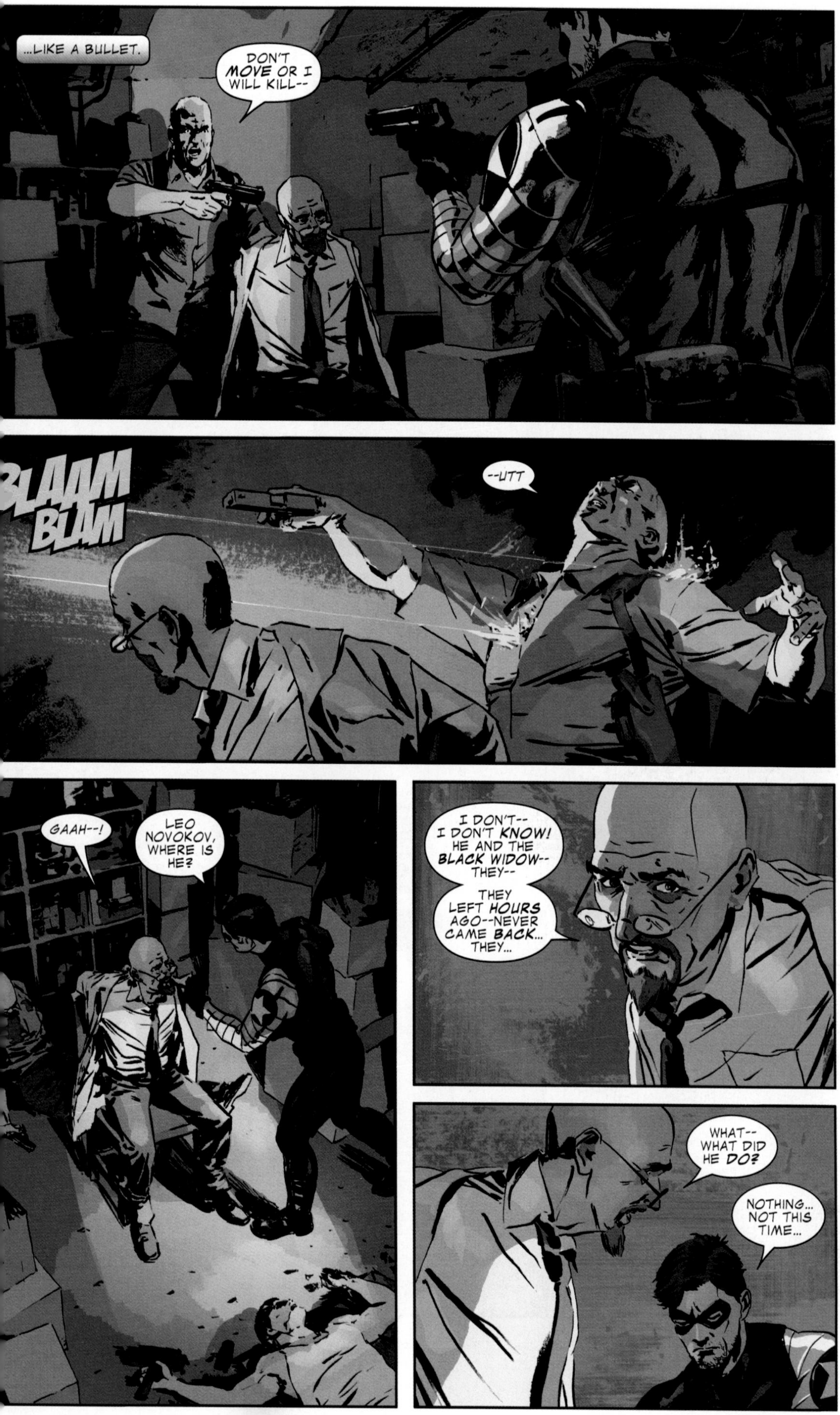
...LIKE A BULLET.
DON'T MOVE OR I WILL KILL--
BLAAM
BLAM
--UTT
GAAH--!
LEO NOVOKOV, WHERE IS HE?
I DON'T-- I DON'T KNOW! HE AND THE BLACK WIDOW-- THEY--
THEY LEFT HOURS AGO--NEVER CAME BACK... THEY...
WHAT-- WHAT DID HE DO?
NOTHING... NOT THIS TIME...

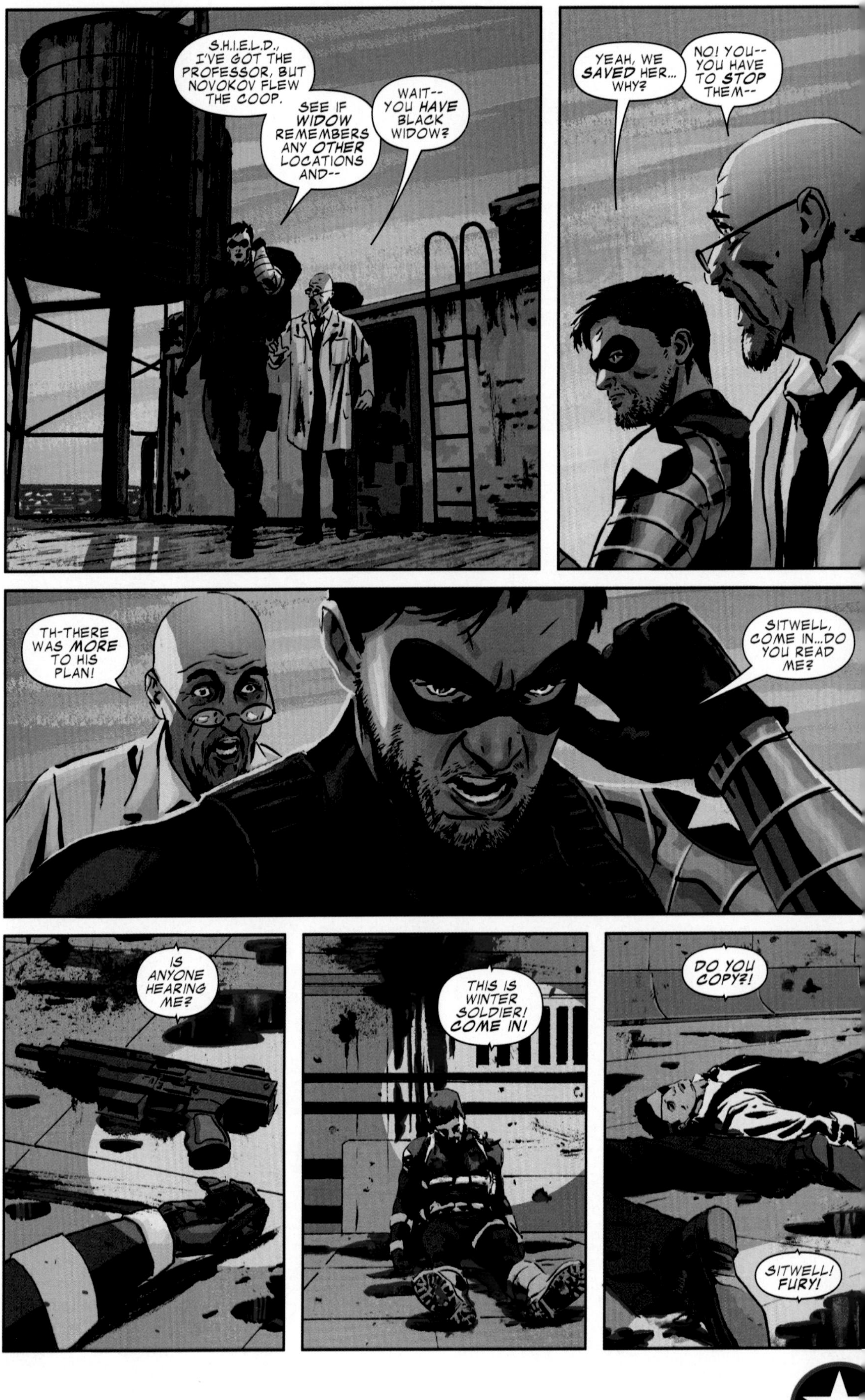
S.H.I.E.L.D., I'VE GOT THE PROFESSOR, BUT NOVOKOV FLEW THE COOP.
SEE IF WIDOW REMEMBERS ANY OTHER LOCATIONS AND--
WAIT-- YOU HAVE BLACK WIDOW?
YEAH, WE SAVED HER... WHY?
NO! YOU-- YOU HAVE TO STOP THEM--
TH-THERE WAS MORE TO HIS PLAN!
SITWELL, COME IN...DO YOU READ ME?
IS ANYONE HEARING ME?
THIS IS WINTER SOLDIER! COME IN!
DO YOU COPY?!
SITWELL! FURY!

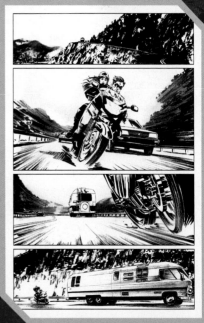

ISSUE #7, PAGE 9

ISSUE #7, PAGE 10

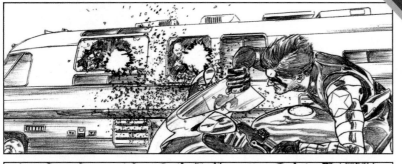

ISSUE #7, PAGE 11

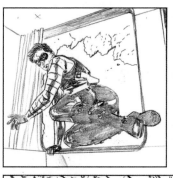

ISSUE #7, PAGE 12

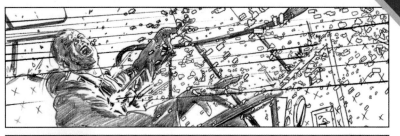

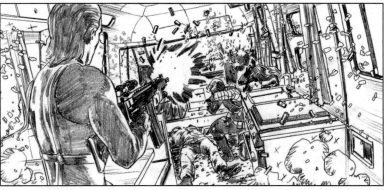

ISSUE #7, PAGE 13

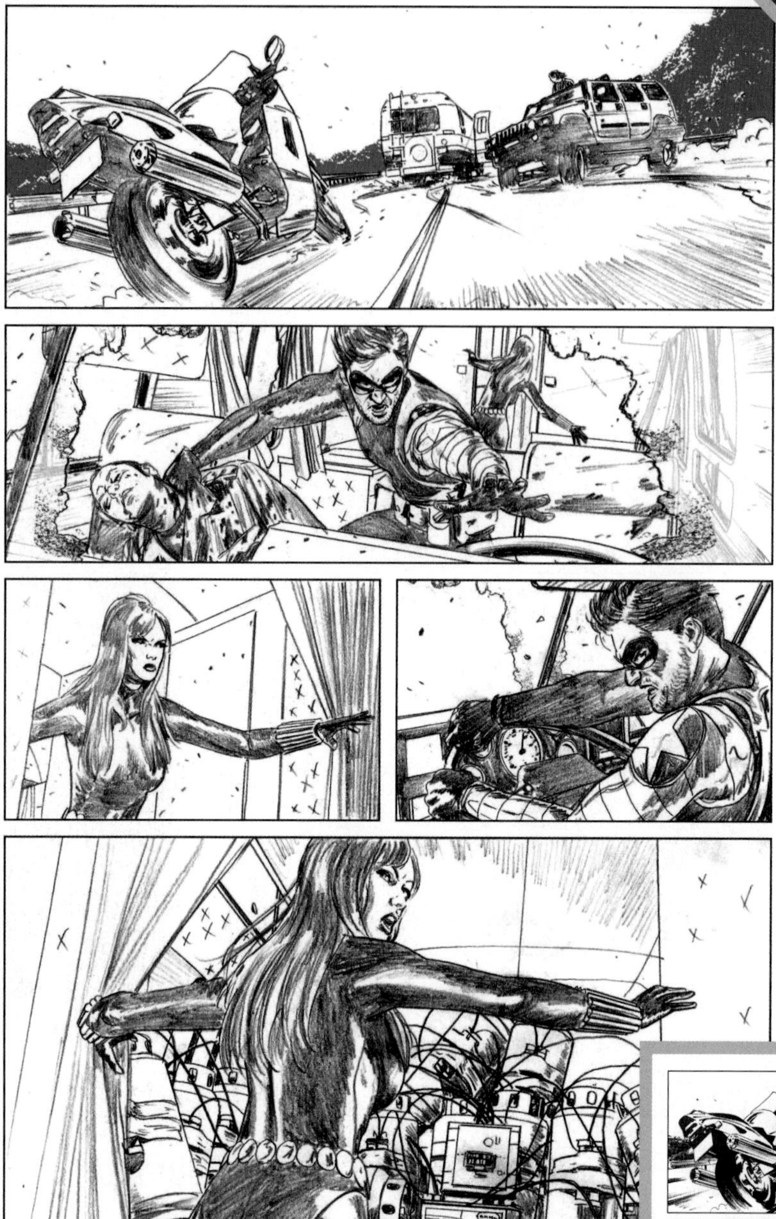

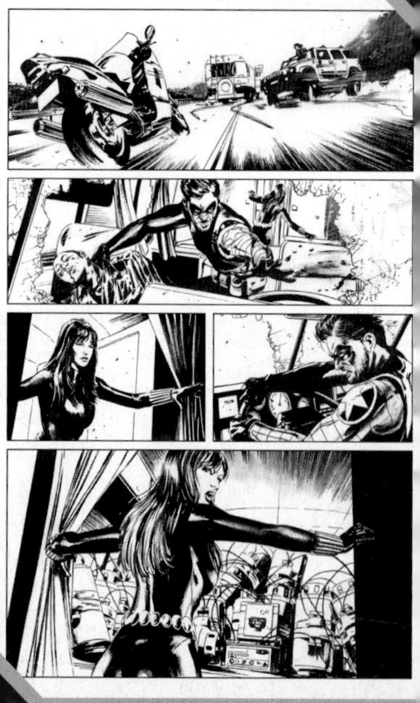

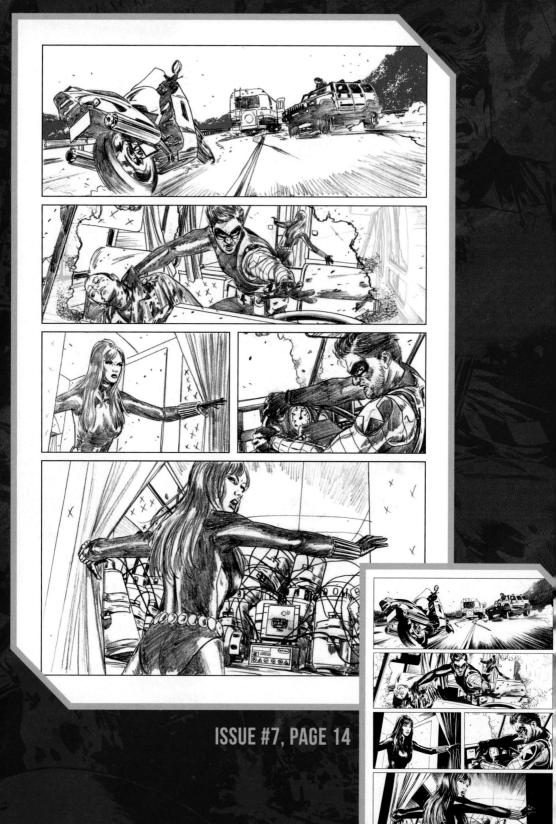

ISSUE #7, PAGE 14

ISSUE #7, PAGE 15

ISSUE #7, PAGE 16